ABOUT THE AUTHORS

David Morrison is a top motivational speaker appearing before such corporate groups across Canada and the US as IBM, Traveler's Insurance, Blue Cross Blue Shield, American Red Cross, BASF, and Eli Lilly, and in management extension programs at colleges and universities. He is an executive coach and the principal of Morrison Motivational Concepts Inc., following a successful career in sales, management, and learning and development, at Olivetti, Citibank, and TD Bank Financial Group. *Email: morrisonmotivational@sympatico.ca*

Syd Kessler is one of North America's top advertising executives, having been the principal of Kessler Productions, Kessler Music Inc., The Air Company, and Supercorp (with John Labatt Ltd.). An investor in Brand Voice Inc., Rocket Boys Inc., and Scientific Intelligence, he is the author of *The Perfect System: Finding Certainty and Purpose in the Science of Life. Email: kess@rogers.com*

VIBES

VIBES

*The Scientific Secret to
Achieving Extraordinary Results
in Sales and Management*

David Morrison
and Syd Kessler

BASTIAN
BOOKS

Bastian Books
A division of Bastian Publishing Services Ltd.
www.bastianpubserv.com

Distributed by Publishers Group Canada
www.pgcbooks.ca

ISBN 0-9780554-0-3

Cataloguing in Publication Data
available from Library and Archives Canada

Editorial: Donald G. Bastian, Bastian Publishing Services Ltd.
www.bastianpubserv.com

Cover and interior design: Daniel Crack, Kinetics Design

Printed and bound in Canada by Webcom

To the
Memory of
John Michael Fry
1984–2004

CONTENTS

Acknowledgments   xi

Introduction   1

A Vibes Questionnaire   6

1 UNDERSTANDING VIBES

1 Everything Is Vibrating Energy   11
2 Thoughts Are Vibes, Too   14
3 How We Broadcast Vibes   21
4 How Vibes Attract   25

2 RAISING YOUR VIBES

5 Use Your Mind Carefully   35
6 Focus Your Mind on a Vision   41
7 Live in the Moment   53
8 Look Up   60

3 SALES AND MANAGEMENT VIBES

9 The Vibes of Companies   69
10 The Vibes of Sales   76
11 The Vibes of Management   89
12 The Vibes of Leadership   104
13 Leadership Vibes and Vision   117

Conclusion   127

CONTENTS

ACKNOWLEDGMENTS

I have many people to thank for their input and support on this journey:

Syd Kessler for his catalytic ideas about life and the science of how the universe works; Martin Tammer of the *National Post* for his early encouragement and help with my writing; and Donald G. Bastian of Bastian Books, who taught me how to write a book.

My wife, Edna, and my children, Brad, Kaelyn, and Breanne, who gave support in many ways and helped with the production side of writing.

Chris Shaughnessy, Peter Norton, Lynn Beglan, Bob Pinkney, and Kevin Tisdale, who shared their personal vibes stories with me.

Phil Scott, who taught me much about the vibes of management and sales.

Mike Saczkowski, Gus Jacacci, Jim Povec, and my brother, Peter, whose comments and encouragement helped shape the book.

Gary Fry, John's father, who provided a model of good-vibes selling.

The hundreds of people in my audiences and focus groups who graciously submitted to hearing my vibes presentations and provided invaluable feedback.

VIBES

INTRODUCTION

In 1966, a rock and roll group, the Beach Boys, had a hit song, "Good Vibrations," which suggested that certain people have "good vibrations" that give "excitations" to others.

At the time, I thought it was about sex. After all, it was four guys singing about a girl.

Fast Forward 40 years, to 2006. Ryan Seacrest, host of the popular TV show _American Idol_, asks a contestant, "So, what kind of vibes do you think the judges are giving off tonight?" The young woman, in her early 20s, understands the question immediately and answers accordingly.

Over those four decades, the phrase "good vibrations," or "good vibes," has evolved to be about much more than sex. Marketing campaigns, sales conferences, vacation destinations, real-estate offerings, business conferences – all have been rolled out under this theme. There is even a car named Vibe, built by Pontiac.

But what exactly is the context of the question in your mind? What would your co-workers, customers, friends, and family say if Ryan asked them about your vibes?

That's what this book is about: discovering the secret of vibes – where they come from within us; how they can either attract others or push them away; and how we can raise them so people are attracted to us.

My Journey

My own discovery of vibes has been part of a lifelong journey. I spent a career in corporate learning and development, both as a teacher and an executive, and thus was involved in many sales and management courses. Although they weren't labeled "Vibes Courses," that, unwittingly to me at the time, was their underlying theme.

Focusing on a series of skills, behaviors, and practices, they taught people how to get customers and employees to feel attracted to their ideas, causes, and products, and say "yes."

If you're a corporate citizen, you've probably been on a couple of these courses. You know the skills and practices being taught often do not deliver on their promise in the real world. This was something that always bothered me, and I spent many years trying to figure out the mystery of how to construct and deliver more effective programs.

Then, a few years ago, the answers began to evolve for me. They came from an unexpected source: science.

I have always had a keen interest in things scientific. Whether through books, programs, or workshops that explain how our universe works, I love trying to make sense of it all.

The last couple of decades have seen major discoveries on a number of fronts, all of which have had a similar theme, that the universe doesn't operate the way our five senses (seeing, hearing, feeling, tasting, and smelling) tell us it does. A lot is going on that we are unaware of because of our limitations.

The more I studied these discoveries, the more I began to think there was more going on when salespeople and managers interacted with others than our senses could detect.

Then, three years ago, I was having lunch with an old friend, Syd Kessler. We were discussing a book he had written, *The Perfect System*. It's about quantum science and getting one's life in sync with the natural laws of the universe. During our discussion, I had the overwhelming feeling that the answers to my sales and management mystery could also be found here. The resulting story of my journey of discovery, this book, is mine, but it wouldn't have been written without Syd's inspiration and guidance.

And, indeed, I have concluded that many insights from the findings of science shed new light on human interaction – insights that, if put into practice, could greatly enhance our ability to attract others.

The Haves and Have-Nots

As I began my career in corporate training, I quickly realized that my audiences were made up of three distinct groups. The first and most populous group contained those who were going to gain some benefit from the course. The second and third groups were at opposite ends of the learning spectrum from each other. One of these groups included those who didn't seem to need the training at all. They were going to be successful no matter what. The other included those who, no matter how hard they tried, were probably never going to be able to create the feelings in employees and customers that were the objective of the course. I came to call these two groups the haves and have-nots.

The have-nots were not necessarily lacking in ability. One person in particular, a new account manager with an ivy-league MBA, amazed me. He took in the selling skills effortlessly. Then, during the role-play sessions, he repeated them flawlessly. Because of this, I followed his career after he left training. I was surprised to learn that in the real world he was totally unable to build any rapport with clients.

In listening to the story of his demise, I was reminded of some people who had worked alongside me during my sales career. No matter how hard they tried, they just couldn't connect to people in a positive way.

In contrast, the haves, the ones who had already been successful, brought uplifting energy to almost everything they did. Clients and co-workers always looked forward to spending time with them, knowing they would feel good as a result.

The Journey Ahead

If you see yourself as part of the majority of people who learn something from company training programs, you will definitely benefit from this book. If you see yourself as a have-not, you will understand why this is so and what you need to do to change things. If you feel you are already a have, you will gain insight into your success from a scientific perspective and will be able to fine-tune your natural abilities.

Vibes is about the mind: how we use it and how it can create an energy field of attraction we can feel in ourselves and transmit to others.

This book will give you insights into yourself and the people you know. It will explain why you like to be around certain people and why you want to hide when you see others heading your way. It will answer the puzzle of the haves and have-nots. It will also give you the answers you need to increase your ability to attract others to your ideas, causes, and products.

Vibes is written in three parts. The first part of the book, "Understanding Vibes," is about some recent discoveries in physics, medicine, and neurobiology that offer new insights into why people feel attracted to some people and not to others.

The second part, "Raising Your Vibes," contains a four-step process for ensuring that you are creating good vibes.

The third part, "Sales and Management Vibes," shares practical applications of the theories to the processes of those two areas.

It is my belief that *Vibes*, in unexpected and dramatic ways, will change the way you interact with co-workers, customers, and the people in your personal life, and will transform your life.

A VIBES QUESTIONNAIRE

Before you read this book, think about your own vibes.

If your family, friends, and co-workers were asked about you, what would they say?

Would they describe you as someone they look forward to spending time with or as someone they sometimes wish to avoid?

The following questionnaire will help you determine your Vibes Quotient (VQ). In filling it out, don't think the answers through – just go with your initial feelings.

On a scale of 1 to 10, score yourself on the following:

1 When going to a reception where you don't know anyone you:

1	2	3	4	5	6	7	8	9	10

Check things out first   Walk up to the first person
to get a feel for the event   you see and start talking

2 On most mornings, your energy level is

1	2	3	4	5	6	7	8	9	10

Less than you would like it to be   Ideal

3 How much of your time do you spend dreaming about a positive future?

1	2	3	4	5	6	7	8	9	10

0%   100%

4 Most people would say that you are usually:

1	2	3	4	5	6	7	8	9	10

Stressed   Relaxed and easygoing

5 When you think about your accomplishments and possessions, you:

1	2	3	4	5	6	7	8	9	10

Speak of them to others with pride   Rarely think about them

6 *How often do you find yourself having worrying thoughts?*

_1_	_2_	_3_	_4_	_5_	_6_	_7_	_8_	_9_	_10_

Quite often   Almost never

7 *Others would say that you try to bring fun into everything you do:*

_1_	_2_	_3_	_4_	_5_	_6_	_7_	_8_	_9_	_10_

Almost never   Always

8 *When presented with a sudden change in plans, your immediate response is to:*

_1_	_2_	_3_	_4_	_5_	_6_	_7_	_8_	_9_	_10_

Look at the problems   Look for the opportunities
it might create   it might provide

9 *Would others say that you think about yourself or others more?*

_1_	_2_	_3_	_4_	_5_	_6_	_7_	_8_	_9_	_10_

Yourself   Others

10 *How often do you give money away?*

_1_	_2_	_3_	_4_	_5_	_6_	_7_	_8_	_9_	_10_

Never   Often

My VQ score _____

Now add up the numbers you circled.

If your VQ score is 80 or above, you're probably seen as a person who attracts others.

If your score is between 40 and 80, you're like most people: sometimes giving off vibes that are attractive to others and sometimes not.

If your score is below 40, well, I think you get the picture.

Now that you have an idea of where you think you stand, read on to find out why this is so, how to create the vibes you want for yourself, and how to send them out to others.

PART 1

Understanding Vibes

"The whole of science is nothing more than a refinement of everyday thinking."
– Albert Einstein

CHAPTER 1

Everything
Is Vibrating
Energy

I am not a scientist, but with the help of others, including some experts, I have gained an understanding that I believe reveals what's happening when people are attracted to others. Something our five senses are unable to detect.

This was validated for me recently when I spoke about the vibes concepts to a large group of executives from a major pharmaceutical company, Eli Lilly, 20 percent of whom were scientists. Afterward, I received a note from the organizers that said, "You certainly raised debate among the scientists. A few thought your interpretations a bit tenuous, but most, including a psychiatrist, agreed wholeheartedly."

The most important revelations in science in the past 100 years have come from quantum science. It is not an easy subject, but the aspects central to what I'm calling vibes are easy to grasp.

The basic premise is that everything in the universe is made up of energy. Your five senses tell you this book in your hands is solid matter, but you are being fooled by their limitations. An electron microscope would show us the molecules making up the paper in this book are made of atoms, each one of which is made of a nucleus with a cloud of electrons pulsating around it. When we use an atom-smasher, such as the two-mile long Linear Accelerator at Stanford University, to see what electrons are made of, we find nucleons (protons and neutrons), which in turn are made up of quarks, a kind of vibrating energy.

A recent theory called string theory suggests that even quarks are made up of something else: stuff that looks like pieces of string or elastic bands but that in fact is nothing but energy. We'll have to wait until the longest atom-smasher ever built is finished in Switzerland in 2008 to find out if this theory is correct.

But whether we talk about quarks or strings doesn't matter. Either way, they are both a form of vibrating energy, and, as scientists agree, everything in the universe, EVERYTHING, is made up of this energy.

Of equal importance is the fact that all this energy is connected. The mathematical aspects of quantum science tell us everything in the universe is connected to everything else. Our five senses may tell us you and I are separate people, but in fact, at a subatomic level, we are connected.

Energy vibrating at lower oscillations (the speed of the vibration from one point to the other), say, ten million times per second, can be perceived by our senses as solid matter or liquids or vapors. We know higher oscillating energies (trillions of times per second) are all around us in the form of radio waves, microwaves, television signals, and x-rays – and these we are blind to.

The idea that everything in the universe is energy, taking different forms, was easy for me to grasp. As a science buff, I had heard it before. The next part of my journey, however, was a complete surprise to me, and I think it will be for you, too.

CHAPTER 2

Thoughts Are Vibes, Too

As I was trying to get my head around the fact that everything in the universe is made up of vibrating energy, it never occurred to me that this would also apply to thoughts. But in fact they are, as a 20-year span of research in kinesiology (the study of muscles and their movement) has proven.

David Hawkins, in his landmark book *Power vs. Force: The Hidden Determinants of Human Behavior*, chronicles the study of kinetic energy in our muscles and how different types of thoughts affect them. He cites a simple experiment proving this concept. I have used it with many audiences when I talk about the concepts of vibes. Try it for yourself, with a friend.

In this exercise, I ask for a volunteer and have them stand facing me, left arm relaxed at their side, right arm held out parallel to the floor, elbow straight. (You may use either the right or left arm.)

I then place my right hand on their left shoulder to steady them. Then I place my left hand on their extended right arm just above the wrist.

Next I request that they resist when I count to three and try to push their arm down.

I push down quickly, evenly, and firmly. The idea is to push just hard enough to test the spring and bounce in the arm, but not so hard that the muscle becomes fatigued. It is not a question of who is stronger but whether the muscle can lock the shoulder joint against the push.

Assuming there isn't any physical problem with the muscle and the subject is in a normal, relaxed state of mind, not receiving any external stimuli, the muscle will test strong.

At this point, I repeat the steps, but this time, with apologies, I ask the subject to focus on something they are worried about, something they are afraid may happen. I ask them to hold the focus for 10 seconds. Then I conduct the test again. Always, the subject has much less strength in the arm. In some cases the arm can be pushed down with almost no resistance (creating a very surprised look on my subject's face).

This exercise and others like it demonstrate that our thoughts do indeed affect the energy in our bodies. Taken even further, the research shows that the energy produced by certain types of thoughts or states of consciousness can be accurately measured and calibrated.

Hawkins writes that over the years of his studies, "Millions of calibrations have defined a range of values accurately corresponding to well recognized sets of attitudes and emotions, localized by specific attractor energy fields, much as electromagnetic fields gather iron filings." He has classified the energy fields "so as to be easily comprehensible as well as clinically accurate."

His measurements calibrate the energy levels produced by the types of thoughts that fill our minds. The scale he uses is 0–1000, with zero being the lowest energy and 1000 the highest. "It's very important to remember that the calibration figures do not represent an arithmetic, but a *logarithmic*, *progression*," he writes. "Thus, the level 300 is not twice the amplitude of 150: it is 10 to the 300th power. An increase of even a few points represents a major advance in power."

In what follows, I have summarized, in my own words, his descriptions of each sate of consciousness. I start with the lowest.

Energy level 20: Shame

We all have some awareness of the pain of losing face, becoming discredited, or feeling like a non-person. We hang our heads in shame and slink away, wishing we were invisible.

Energy Level 30: Guilt

Many struggle with guilt their entire lives. Guilt domination results in a preoccupation with sin. Guilt is an unforgiving emotional attitude that some use for coercion and control.

Energy Level 50: Apathy

This level is characterized by poverty, despair, and hopelessness. The world and the future look bleak. It is a state of helplessness.

Energy Level 75: Grief

This is sadness, loss, and dependency, the level of mourning, bereavement, and remorse about the past.

Energy Level 100: Fear

At the level of 100, a lot more life energy is available. Fear of danger is healthy. But when fear is one's focus, the endless worrisome events of the world feed it. Fear limits growth of personality and leads to inhibition.

Energy Level 125: Desire

Desire motivates vast areas of human activity, including the economy. Desire also has to do with accumulation and greed. It can become the energy level of addiction. The desire for attention can drive others away with its constant demands.

Energy Level 150: Anger

Anger expresses itself most often as resentment and revenge and is therefore volatile and dangerous. While it does produce energy, that energy is usually short-lived and, in the end, debilitating.

Energy Level 175: Pride

Pride has enough energy to run the United States Marine Corps. But we all know that "pride goeth before a fall." Pride is defensive and vulnerable because it is dependent on external conditions. The inflated ego is vulnerable to attack, which can lead to shame or anger.

Energy Level 200: Courage

What Hawkins calls "Power Energy" first appears at the level 200. It is the level of empowerment, which is the zone of exploration, accomplishment, fortitude, and determination. Courage implies the willingness to try new things. In contrast, at lower levels of energy, the world is seen as hopeless, sad, frightening, or frustrating, all of which are energy-draining states of mind.

Energy Level 250: Neutrality

This energy level can be very positive because it is epitomized by release from the positionality that typifies lower levels. To be neutral means to be relatively unattached to outcomes, to roll with the punches. The neutral position allows for flexibility and belief that whatever happens will be the right thing.

Energy Level 310: Willingness

At the level of willingness, work is done well and success in all endeavors is common. Willingness implies that one has overcome inner resistance to life and is committed to participation. Willing people are builders and contributors to society.

Energy Level 350: Acceptance

Here a major transformation takes place, with the understanding that one is the source and creator of the experience of one's life. People below 200 tend to be powerless and see themselves as victims at the mercy of life.

Energy Level 400: Reason

Intelligence and rationality rise to the forefront when the emotionalism of the lower levels is transcended. This is the level of science, medicine, and of a generally increased capacity for conceptualization and comprehension. Understanding and information are the main tools of accomplishment.

Energy Level 500: Love

This level is not about love as depicted in the mass media. The 500 level is characterized by a love that is unconditional, unchanging, and permanent. Love is a state of being.

It is a forgiving, nurturing, and supportive way of relating to the world. Love focuses on the goodness of life and all its expressions.

Energy Level 540: Joy

As love becomes less conditional, it begins to be experienced as inner joy. Joy arises from within each moment of existence rather than from any other source. It has an extraordinary capacity for patience and persistence, fueling a positive attitude in the face of prolonged adversity.

Energy Level 600: Peace

A continuous energy field of peace is associated with the experience of transcendence, self-realization, and God-consciousness. It is extremely rare, attained by very few. Some of these people appear saintly and a few are even designated as such.

Energy Level 700–1000: Enlightenment

This is the level of the great ones in history who originated the spiritual patterns that countless people have followed throughout the ages. All are associated with, and often identified with, divinity. This is the level of powerful inspiration; these beings set in place attractor energy fields that influence all of humankind.

Hawkins's work has been cited as being landmark in terms of how we understand the energy of our thoughts. From it, it's easy to see why asking my volunteers to focus on thoughts of worry or fear, all below the 200 level (courage), drained the energy from their bodies. Hawkins states, "All levels of thought below 200 are destructive of life in both the individual and society at large; all levels above 200 are constructive expressions of power and energy."

The decisive level of 200 is the fulcrum that divides true sustaining energy from that given to us by such things as anger and fear and even pride, which are short-lived and debilitating.

Hawkins also states that the levels of consciousness are always mixed, with people operating at even markedly different levels in different areas of life.

Most people find their thoughts can be all over the Hawkins scale at any given moment. We can be having good-vibe thoughts, above 200, only to be dragged down to gut grinds a second later.

As we will see in the second part of this book, on how you can raise your vibes, the secret is to monitor our thoughts and their energy level and to try to keep them above the 200 level at all times.

My journey had now provided two insights. First, everything is energy, and, second, the energy level of our thoughts can be calibrated. So far, I didn't have any real insights into the energy (vibes) of attraction, but the next step in the journey began to pull things together.

Some of the references cited by Hawkins and other scientists indicated that not only is the energy in the muscles of our body affected by our thoughts, so, too, is the electrostatic energy field surrounding our bodies. And that this field plays an important part in the attraction of others to our thoughts.

CHAPTER 3

How We Broadcast Vibes

The references to our electrostatic energy field led me to the work of science writer Itzak Bentov, who, in his book, *Stalking the Wild Pendulum*, writes:

> As long as we are alive, our bodies produce an electrostatic field around themselves, a field that can be easily measured by commercially available static meters. The strength of the static field depends very much on the vitality of the subject. A person brimming with energy will produce a big signal while one whose vitality is low will produce practically no signal at all.

It also led me to the work of Dr. Valerie Hunt, who holds advanced degrees in psychology and physiological science. She teaches at Columbia and the University of California. In her book *Infinite Mind*, Hunt presents a comprehensive human energy field model based on 25 years of electronic field research and extensive clinical studies. She writes: "Although we cannot explain life, we do know that electrical activity is essential for it. Pasteur found that electrical polarization distinguishes living matter from dead matter even though the chemical compositions were identical."

An electroencephalogram (EEG) can measure electrical energy produced by the brain. Brainwaves under normal conditions produce a characteristic slow waveform, from zero to 20 cycles per second. The heart, measured by an electrocardiogram (EKG), creates a larger and faster wave up to 225 cycles per second, while muscles, measured by an electromyogram (EMG), have a wide range, from zero up to 250 cycles per second in small, fast-moving eye muscles.

Collectively, these energies have been called many things, including aura, chakra, chi, prana, odic force, and life force. Hunt prefers the simple term "energy field." The fact that these energies have caught the attention of so many belief systems over the centuries suggests that at an intuitive level we have always known they exist and most of us have had some kind of experience of them.

We All Broadcast Vibes to Others

Most of us have had the experience of feeling the broadcast of others' energy fields. Often it happens like this: We're at a reception or other public gathering having a conversation with a small group, and suddenly we have a strong sense we are under another's gaze. We respond automatically, without thinking, 90 percent of the time turning in the exact direction of the stare. Somehow we are able to detect the energy and the direction it is coming from. Most of us have also been caught on the broadcast end of this exchange. We see an interesting character and find ourselves turning away, embarrassed, when our staring catches the person's attention.

Wayne Dyer, a psychologist and author of many books, talks about our ability to tap people. He proves his ability to friends by having them pick out someone across the street walking into view. He then concentrates thoughts and fixes his gaze on the individual. The bet is that before they walk out of sight, they will turn in his direction, looking for the source of the energy, without knowing why. Apparently he wins almost every time, and apparently anyone can do this with a little practice.

There is definitely something going on here that our senses cannot detect. Somehow the energy fields produced by the stare and the thoughts are being broadcast and received by others. If we follow our early premise that everything is vibrating energy and everything is connected, this should not surprise us.

Hunt offers an explanation from her research:

> Thought is an organized field of energy composed of complex patterns of vibrations which consolidate information. If the accompanying emotional energy is strong, the field is energetic and integrated. It persists and stimulates other fields to action, both in matter and other human beings.

The term "in matter" could well be the topic of a whole other book, but for now we'll focus on the living aspect of all this.

Hunt's research shows that human energy fields display a continuum. The extremely low frequency vibrations (ELF) are directly involved with life's biological processes. The extremely high frequency vibrations (EHF) ally with the mind-field and awareness and are similar for all people, often producing vibrations in the range of 200,000 cycles per second.

Hunt writes that energy fields appear to interact with each other within the animal kingdom. Writing of Jacques Cousteau's reports of sharks off beaches in Australia and France attacking the same person, she asks: "Do human fields, then, attract sharks … ? Marine research shows that dolphins and sharks respond to vibrational frequencies up to 200,000 cycles per second, the same range we recorded from some human fields."

She also points out that domestic animals are attracted to people with "higher vibratory fields."

For me, another proof that animals are capable of picking up vibrational frequencies that humans cannot, came the day after Christmas 2004. That was when the tsunami hit the coastal communities of Indonesia, Sri Lanka, India, and Thailand. More than 300,000 people were killed, yet not one wild animal carcass was found, anywhere, not one. Aware of vibes that humans could not sense, the animals sought higher ground.

At this point, answers were beginning to fall into place for me and a pattern was emerging. But an important piece was still missing.

I understood that everything is vibrating energy and that people's thoughts directly affect the vibes within them. I understood that those vibes were connected to other people's vibes and that our broadcast of them to others had a scientific explanation. What was missing for me was why and how those vibes could have an effect on others and create a pattern of energy that, like a magnet, drew people to them. As surprising as it may seem, fireflies and grandfather clocks provided the answers.

CHAPTER 4

How Vibes Attract

Of the ways energy connects, the one critical to the vibes of attraction is called entrainment. Science confirms for us that vibrations are attracted to one another in particular ways. In *Stalking the Wild Pendulum*, Itzak Bentov describes "rhythm entrainment." This, he says, may be seen in how fireflies flying in a field will blink in a seemingly random fashion. But when they land in a bush, in close proximity to one another, they will begin blinking in unison within a few minutes.

And it's not just true of bug life. Bentov goes on to describe what happens to a roomful of grandfather clocks, hanging on the wall, after their pendulums have been started one after the other:

> When you leave the room you will hear a cacophony of ticking and tocking. If you re-enter the room a few days later, however, what do you think you will hear? A perfect syncopation, all ticking and tocking together, the pendulums will swing to and fro as one.

Bentov writes that, "the tiny amount of energy ... transmitted through the wall from clock to clock is sufficient for rhythm entrainment to occur."

The Most Important Point in This Book

The most important point in this book is that it is the higher- (or faster-) vibrating energy that entrains lower (or slower) energy and brings it up to match it.

The fastest-blinking firefly and the fastest-swinging pendulum cause the others to speed up and match their higher vibrating oscillations.

This explains why we like to be around people whose thought energy is at a higher level on the Hawkins scale, above 200. Our energy level is entrained and brought up to the level of theirs. And since higher-energy thoughts make us feel better, we are happier when we are with them.

For me, the smile is a simple example of human entrainment. Not the smile we give when we are genuinely pleased about something, or the forced smile we produce when we believe it is expected, but the smile we create at will, one others can't escape.

Try this little experiment. Pick someone and tell them you are going to make them smile. Then create a smile of your own, beam it at them, and hold their gaze. As you do, you will feel positive energy in your body; your smile will create it. More importantly, you will find that the other person will begin to smile as well. They have no choice, even if they are "feeling down at the moment," because the higher energies of your facial expression, feelings, and thoughts (smiles come from thoughts above the 200 level) will entrain them.

Just as in the case of the fireflies and the pendulums, their energy level will be attracted to yours. As it is, they not only will match your facial expression, but they will also feel the same energy in their body you do.

Trying to make people cry by crying at them, however, almost never works. The lower energy of sadness will not entrain others unless they are already feeling down.

We Have All Tried to Entrain Others

The concept of entrainment isn't new to any of us; it's just the term that we may not have heard. We have all found ourselves trying to bring other people "up" at one time or another.

When others are sad, whether over the death of a loved one, the loss of a job, a sickness, or traffic accident, we find ourselves saying something to the effect of, "Now now, don't worry. I know how you feel, but trust me, it will get better." Some see this as an unrealistic or even insincere thing to say, and it is true most of us want to avoid or change bad thoughts because they drain our energy. However, there is a sincere reason behind our saying such things: we don't like to see others suffer and want to bring them back up to a state of higher energy. Science now explains this phenomenon.

We Can Easily Feel the Attraction of Others

I often ask my audiences, "Who is the one person in the world you like to be with most?" I then ask them to write down the reasons why. You may want to do the same right now before reading further.

Compare your list with the answers I receive from my groups. I believe you'll see a lot of similarity.

Makes me feel good

Makes me feel good about myself

Loves me unconditionally

Does not judge me

Cares greatly for me

Makes me laugh

Listens to me with genuine interest

Is open to my ideas

I also ask them to list of reasons why they don't like to be around other people. Responses include:

Very self-interested

Always complaining about things

Greedy

Judgmental

Angry at the world

Talk mostly about themselves

People are able to easily differentiate between those who send out attraction energy and those who send out the opposite. They also find it easy to give the reasons. If you look at the two lists and then refer back to the Hawkins scale (see Chapter 2), it will be obvious to you which list fits on which side of the 200 level.

Doesn't the person you are attracted to live most often in the vicinity of positive thoughts above 200, thoughts focused on others, on you? And doesn't the person you are least attracted to think mostly below 200, and mostly about themselves?

How do people feel when they are around you? Do your thoughts lift and energize others? We'll look at this question in more detail later, but for now ask yourself, "Do I spend most of my thinking time above or below the 200 level?"

Gravitating to a Higher Purpose

I find it interesting that when people are given the opportunity to free themselves from thinking about everyday life, most choose to seek out higher-energy levels of thought.

When I was researching this book, I asked groups of managers to reveal what they would do if they had the power to change anything about the world – anything at all, whether in science, industry, politics, commerce, religion, family life, sports, or their jobs. The exercise called on them to create a little model from craft materials and then share their responses with others.

Some spoke passionately of eliminating hunger or eradicating disease, others of doing something for world peace. There were tears in the crowd as people listened to colleagues whom they had never seen in this light. The emotion came because people were exchanging thoughts from the high-energy levels of love, joy, and peace, and of helping others.

When I first used this exercise, years ago, I was surprised to find that seasoned business people did not focus on changing things in their workaday realm. Over the years, very few people, out of the hundreds I have done this with, have ever revealed thoughts of changing things for their own gain.

I continue to use this exercise today. When I ask participants how they felt as they built their models, everyone agrees their feelings were full of very high, positive energy.

At the end of our time together, I share with them the history of the exercise. I tell them how I came across it in leadership-development research years ago as a way to help people explore their leadership potential. I tell them the name of the exercise, "Having a Higher Purpose."

Even though the groups don't know the original context of the exercise, they always gravitate to the theme of Higher Purpose. Some force within us naturally wants to seek this energy out.

There can be a bad side to this. Another mystery solved for me while writing this book was why we refer to the effect of alcohol or drugs as "getting high." Getting stoned, blasted, or wasted, yes, but why "high"? According to Hawkins's research, the answer lies in the fact that the addictive qualities of drugs and alcohol are not in the substances themselves but in the high-energy feelings they produce: the feelings that come from the levels of love, joy, and peace.

These feelings are so powerful that reproducing them can become obsessive. If some people can't get them naturally, they will try to produce them artificially. Twelve-step programs such as Alcoholics Anonymous are designed to help people attain the good feelings without the substance abuse.

Similarly, sales and management people to whom I gave early drafts of this book told me about a pronounced difference in the way their clients, co-workers, friends, and family felt about them after they began practicing good-vibe attitudes and thinking processes.

That's what the next chapters of this book are about: how to practice good vibes. These chapters go over a simple four-step process, one that will definitely change your vibes in a way you'll be able to feel. More importantly, others will notice, too, and you will become the person the Beach Boys sang about.

PART 2

Raising Your Vibes

_"New discoveries in science ... will continue
to create a thousand new frontiers
for those who would still adventure."_
– Herbert Hoover

CHAPTER 5

Use Your Mind Carefully

Although our minds are the most important faculty we have for getting through life, incredibly, we receive no formal training in how to use them. Think of it, a device more powerful than the largest computer and there's no user's manual. And it could really use one because, for the most part, it is extremely uncontrollable. The mind goes anywhere it wants to, anytime it wants to. You can be trying to concentrate on something important, only to be interrupted by thoughts and images of last night's party, or how your boss will react when you give him some bad news tomorrow.

I once read that if we had to rely on our minds to get us across a busy street, we would probably never make it. Halfway there, random thoughts would divert us and get us killed.

The Realm of Worrying

For many of us, the thing the mind diverts to most often is the realm of worrying.

If you're like most of the people I talked to in my research, you probably think worrying is normal. For example, we believe the time we spend worrying about the health and safety of our children is proportionate to their actual health and safety. The fretting makes us feel we are good parents, and we believe it actually ensures our kids' survival. But remember, the thoughts of worry do not produce much energy. They come from below the 200 level on the Hawkins scale, and we know they cause stress and can lead to illness.

How many hours in your lifetime have you devoted to worry? More importantly, how many of the things you worried about came true even close to the way you worried about them? If you're like most people, very few. Most often what we worry about doesn't happen at all. And when something we worry about *does* happen, it usually doesn't produce the consequences that kept us up half the night. Sometimes the situations even turn out to be positive by teaching us a life lesson.

I remember one night in particular when I was unable to sleep because of worry. I was 23 years old. I had discovered credit cards a few years earlier. Now the collection agencies were after me in full cry and I thought my life was over. Looking back on it, I realize that this was one of the best experiences in my life. I made some arrangements to settle up and the lesson I learned about personal credit has sustained me to this day.

So why do we spend so much time there? Since we have never been taught how to think, we have been left to our own devices to figure it out, and we think it's natural. Most people do it, after all. But if our thoughts are responsible for our body's energy and electrostatic field, surely it is important for us to understand this aspect of life. After all, we all want as much energy as possible in order to live our lives to the fullest.

We make choices about how we spend the moments of our days, and, in the broader picture, our lives. Why not use thinking to our advantage? We can have a choice about the thoughts we think. We can choose to approach problems from energy levels below 200, or from the higher ones. It just takes a little practice.

Reframing

We can all recognize when a thought below level 200 enters our mind. We can feel the tenseness, the constriction, in our bodies. We know it doesn't feel as good as the thoughts above 200 do. We also know we have the power to change the thought – for example, by thinking of a piece of chocolate cake, right now.

Let's say we're worried about a bill payment. We're watching TV and the worrisome thought comes flying in. If we don't change the thought, other worrisome thoughts around the same issue attach themselves. "If Charlie would only pay me back the money he owes me this wouldn't be a problem." And then, "Darn that Charlie anyway, he's always doing this. He did the same thing two years ago – why do I let myself get taken in?" Before we know it, we have spent three or four minutes spiraling down in our energy level. Eventually, we snap out of it because we realize what we are doing, but by that time, the damage to our energy level has been done.

Instead, as we recognize the bad-vibes thought, we should reframe it to something like: "This bill will be paid! I don't know exactly how right now, but like every other problem I've ever worried about, this too shall pass. I'll get through it somehow and look back wondering why I gave it the time of day."

Practice this way of reframing your thoughts for a few days. You will be amazed by the amount of energy you will begin to feel in your body and mind. This will happen because you will have refused to allow negative, energy-draining thoughts to take hold.

But be aware of the word "practice." It is more than it seems. We've all heard the old joke about the tourist in New York City who asks someone on the street, "How do I get to Carnegie Hall?" only to be told, "Practice, practice, practice!"

If you have ever tried to learn how to play a musical instrument or taken lessons in playing a sport, you will know that at first the new physical movement does not feel comfortable. You have to practice until it becomes ingrained in muscle memory. Only then will it feel natural.

The same is true of our thought processes. It may seem very simple to say, "Just change your thinking," but if we have been in the habit of worrying and thinking thoughts below the 200 level for years, changing those patterns will feel uncomfortable at first.

With practice, however, it will become second nature.

Try this experiment. Every time you feel a negative thought come into your mind (remember, you feel it in your body), reframe it as I suggested in connection with my bill-payment problem. At first you will find yourself sliding back into spiral-down thinking. Don't be discouraged. As with a golf swing or the new guitar chord, if you keep at it, it will soon become natural. You will be surprised by the upswing in your emotions.

Vision

There is another, very important reason why reframing thoughts is such a powerful concept. When you reframe your problems you are also creating a positive, higher-energy "desired future state," a *vision*, regarding the issue. This is one of the most important tools people have at their disposal for utilizing the energy of attraction. There are many books about it, and it has been called many things: guided imagery, creative visualization, future state thinking, imagineering. It all comes down to having a vision. That's what you are doing when you think, "This bill will be paid." You are creating an image in your mind of a positive desired future state above 200: a *vision*.

Reframing thoughts also works well in management strategy sessions. I was working with a group who were meeting to solve a problem that had come their way. They were executives of what had been the highest-producing region of a large company and were meeting to figure out why they had fallen from first to fourth place so quickly.

They had asked me to start the day off with something motivating and uplifting, something that would energize them for the rest of their deliberations. At the time, I had just finished my research into Hawkins's energy levels of thoughts and decided to try the concepts out on them. Not only were they engaged by the information, but in thanking me for my presentation, the senior vice president commented that without this information they would have approached the rest of the day from the levels of pride and shame, perhaps even from grief and anger. Now, she said, they would refocus their approach to come from the levels of acceptance, willingness, reason, and courage – levels producing much more energy for creative thinking than those below 200.

What she and her colleagues did was "change their channel," and you can change yours, too. Just flip the switch in your mind.

CHAPTER 6

Focus Your Mind on a Vision

Jack Nicklaus, in his book *Golf My Way*, says he never hit a shot, *not even in practice*, without first creating three pictures in his mind of what the shot would look like when finished. Even down to the detail of the ball's bounces on landing.

The Power of Vision

Every one of us has used vision at one time or another in our lives. We buy a new home and are standing with our spouse looking at the existing backyard. "You know, honey," we say, "I think if we take out that old cedar hedge, replace it with a nice lattice fence, and put a stone patio in that corner ..." What we are doing is creating a picture in our mind of a desired future state. And very often, the backyard ends up looking just as we imagined.

Whether it's a golf shot, backyard, a new car, a great vacation, or a birthday party to surprise a loved one, we all have dreams or visions of what we want to have happen. Now the sciences of psychology and quantum mechanics are giving us insight into to why it works.

The most defining element of my life is the fact that as a young boy, I developed a chronic stammer. It t-t-t-t-t-took m-m-m-me l-l-longer to say t-t-t-t-hings than people had time to listen.

It was defining because overcoming it came to determine my life's journey. Today I speak to audiences all over the world. My guide on that journey was the power of vision.

My stutter got worse over the years, and by high school, it was quite pronounced (no pun intended). For some reason, I accepted my lot in life. Although I saw a therapist once a month, for the most part I did not give it much thought. Until grade 11 history class, at Westdale Collegiate in Hamilton, Ontario.

There I met David Grey, a teacher who with his oratory made history come alive for me and the rest of the class. (He went on to become a professor at a major university and many years later I called to thank him.) He fascinated me. Between classes, I would bring to mind images of him standing before the class, speaking so eloquently. The images played in my head for hours before I fell asleep at night.

At first the images were of him, then they were of me, teaching and speaking in those confident rhythms.

I didn't know it at the time, but I was creating a vision, a picture of a desired future state. In the vision, I was the teacher and speaker. I played this vision so often, I triggered the process that makes visions come true.

I learned about the language and particulars of this process in the mid-1980s when I was doing leadership research and someone gave me some audiotapes by a Dr. Van Vourhees, a professor at Northeastern University. As I listened to him explain his theories, I immediately saw the similarity between what he was saying and my own journey.

The Theory of Vision

The theory is that the subconscious mind has a unique quality. It is unable to distinguish fact from fiction, truth from lie, for some reason always defaulting to truth. It believes everything we are experiencing to be true.

For example, let's say you are watching a sad movie in which a child is dying, Your conscious mind knows full well the child is an actor and the movie is based on a novel. But your subconscious mind believes the child really is dying, so you feel the emotion well up within you (your subconscious controls feelings and emotions) and you shed a few tears.

Immediately, your conscious mind begins to chatter, "Don't cry, you look silly. It's only a movie. Stop blubbering." Since the subconscious only sees the scene once, it is eventually convinced by your chatter, and the feelings subside. However, if it sees something often enough, even if it isn't true, no amount of conscious chatter can deter it. Eventually it locks onto "the truth" and believes the picture is reality.

But it isn't, and that sets up something called "cognitive dissonance." The subconscious hates discord, so it goes to work to make the picture come true, thus bringing harmony to the mind.

How does it do this?

First, it creates focus and energy. Take my stuttering affliction, for example. My images of being a great speaker had been played in my head so often, my subconscious went to work on the assignment. Until that time, I had accepted my stammer, but within six months of hearing David Grey, I found myself wanting to read every book on stammering, linguistics, and speech pathology I could find. I sought out other stammerers and better speech therapists. And I became consumed by the exercises they assigned me.

Second, the subconscious gives you the courage to try new things that will aid you in the journey. For me, one was to sing all my conversations for a time. The good news about this exercise was I didn't stammer when I sang (it is a fact that people who stammer do not do so when singing). The bad news was I didn't have many dates during this period. However, I did find out I could sing, so I never regretted this period of my life.

Third, the subconscious defines a path that draws you along. One of my therapists suggested I choose a career in which speaking was critical. He suggested a job in sales as a start. My subconscious said yes without skipping a beat. While the first few months were hell, I began to realize that many people bought from me simply because I stammered. I went on to become a top producer and sales manager.

Fourth, the subconscious provides you with the answers, words, and thoughts you need to solve the problems you will face on your journey.

Have you ever wondered where your creative thoughts come from? What the origin is of the answers to problems that just pop into your head, or the things you find yourself saying at just the right moment? It's your subconscious, and that's why you usually feel a little tingle as you experience them – they're good and they feel good.

My subconscious certainly gave me the voice and the words in one of my defining moments.

Demonstrating business equipment – mechanical calculators and typewriters – to customers was an important part of the sales process in my first job with Olivetti. Making them look easy to use was key to the sale, but it took a lot of practice because we had to stand behind the equipment and do everything in reverse (the customer was seated in front).

At one point, the district VP, known for his fiery temper, went on a tear because he felt the company's sales standards had fallen. He gave notice he would be visiting the branches, randomly choosing salespeople to show their stuff. "They had better be (expletive deleted) good," he said.

Because of my stammer, I was terrified. Sure enough, on the day in question, the name pulled out of the hat was mine – to the glee of my compatriots, who thought they were in for a good show.

It was one of the most amazing moments of my life, but I can only remember fragments of it. Everything was a blur. I was in a zone, somewhere else. Apparently, I made the machine "dance." Everything worked to perfection and then some. What's more, to my buddies' amazement, I hardly stammered at all. The audience, including Tom, sat there transfixed and at the end broke out into hearty applause.

I now know that my subconscious mind had taken over and guided my hands and words. Here was a chance for me to be recognized as a good speaker, and my subconscious was not going to waste it.

I have talked to many people who have shared a similar experience. Athletes actually call it "being in the zone," a place where time stands still and the performance transcends past abilities.

Tom promoted me to sales manager a few days later. I was told it was a direct result of my performance, and I know it was a defining moment in my life. It was the first time I had ever given a presentation to a group in a business setting, and it had been almost flawless.

Fifth, the subconscious attunes you to opportunities and circumstances that can help make the vision come true. After a successful sales career in office equipment, I went into banking. I was selling asset-based finance for Citibank when I overheard a coffee conversation about the company's new account-manager course. Without knowing why, I found myself joining in.

A few weeks later, I heard Human Resources was looking for a few employees to co-teach the program with professional trainers. Again, my subconscious said yes. Shortly after, I found myself in Boston with Harvard people learning how to conduct the program.

By this time, my stammer was beginning to abate and I had become a fairly good presenter. So much so that I scored in the top 20 percent of the faculty and was chosen to lead the initial senior executive programs of my company, Citibank, in South America and the Pacific Rim.

So there I was, shortly afterward, sitting in the Lufthansa first-class lounge waiting to board a flight to Rio, 17 years to the month from when I first walked into David Grey's class-room. My subconscious had made the vision come true.

Envisioning a Future State

Since coming to an understanding of the theory, I have used the power of vision in almost all aspects of my life. I always create images of my desired future state, whether I'm dealing with long-term goals, such as financial security, or short-term ones, such as the next speech I'm going to give.

When I began writing this book, the first thing I did was sit down and create four mental pictures. I played these in my mind's eye every day and this vision exercise has had the desired effect. The first was seeing the book in print and on the shelves. The second was seeing myself at a book signing. The third was of me speaking about the concepts at conferences (which began to come true before the book was finished). The fourth was of people sitting reading it, as you are doing now.

Ask people who have had a long journey toward a dream, whether a doctor, an astronaut, a scientist, or an entrepreneur with an idea, and they will tell you they had the vision of their success and followed it through. I have spoken on this topic for many years and have heard countless stories. I will say more about vision in the third part of this book, on the vibes of sales and management.

Now that you have read about the power of vision (there are countless books on the topic out there if you want to dig deeper), the question is how to create your own vision. That is the topic we turn to now: taking something that you are worried about or wanting to accomplish and reframing it into a vision that will make your desired future state come true.

Creating and Practicing Visions

As Jack Nicklaus said, he never hit a shot without first playing pictures of it in his mind. As though it had already happened. As you think about your desired future state for something, you must create pictures in your mind as though it has already happened.

It is critical to make the subconscious mind believe that what it is "seeing" is already true.

Some argue that picturing a desired future state is similar to praying for such a state. (Greg Braden, a popular new age thinker, has written a book about this called *The Lost Mode of Prayer*.) In speaking about these ideas at conferences, I am amazed by the number of people who share examples from their religion.

In Christianity there are many passages in the Bible similar to Mark 11:24: "Whatever you ask in prayer, believe that you have received it, and it will be yours."

Not, for example, "Please make me a better husband," but, believing it has already happened, "I am becoming a strong, loving husband."

Or consider Islam. A young man at one of my conferences told a story of focusing on certain passages in the Koran to guide him in envisioning the details of a trip to find a lost brother – to envision them as if they were true. And he was successful in his quest.

As an aside, much of my research and that of others indicates that for the first time in history, the new discoveries in the sciences are beginning to say the same things many religions have been saying for centuries, just in a different way. But that's for another book.

How to Do It

So here's how to create and practice a vision. I'll use weight loss as an example because I have had personal experience of this.

In 1996, after too many years of conference food, I found myself to be 48 pounds overweight. Even on a frame of 6'4", that shows. My doctor, predictably, I suppose, said I had a cholesterol problem.

Rather than going on a diet and exercise program, however, I decided to use the power of vision on this problem. I created five pictures of me at my ideal weight, 200 pounds. In these pictures:

- *I was speaking to a group, and my clothes were hanging perfectly on my frame.*

- *I was winning a tennis match because I was more agile.*

- *I was looking down at the bathroom scale and the dreaded needle was pointing at 200 pounds.*

The two remaining pictures were of me being more attractive to my wife and ... well, you get the idea.

Next, I attached feelings and emotions to the pictures. (Remember, our subconscious loves them and will work to overcome our cognitive dissonance.) As Oprah Winfrey states in the July 2003 issue of *O Magazine*: "Think and feel yourself there. To achieve any aim in life, you need to project the end-result. Think of the elation, the satisfaction, the joy! Carrying the ecstatic feeling will bring the desired goal into view."

In the beginning, every time I was reminded of my weight – when my shirts felt tight or I was out of breath – I simply reframed the thought and brought the desired images to my mind. After I became comfortable with them, I played these images at stoplights, in elevators, and when waiting for meetings to begin.

In some visions, the cognitive dissonance is overcome fairly quickly. The first time I noticed this was a few months later when I came down to the breakfast buffet at a posh conference center and found myself wandering into foreign territory: the fruits and cereals section. I had walked right past the scrambled eggs and sausages, and also the eggs benedict, all of which were previously like magnets to me. I was surprised but quickly realized what was happening.

Within 18 months, I was at 200 pounds, without ever missing any of the foods I had loved so much, and seemingly without a conscious plan for getting there.

Being 200 pounds is now a maintenance vision. I play the pictures every once in a while and never give another thought to food. If I'm hungry, I eat, and if I'm not, I don't. My weight hasn't deviated any more than five pounds either side of 200 since the moment I put my subconscious in charge.

Using Vision

You can do this for any desired future state – as long as that state is within reason. For example, I could envision myself playing in the NBA, but at my age and playing ability it would never happen. I do know I would become a better basketball player as a result of the attempt, though.

Being a sales success, an effective manager, a better spouse, a financial winner, almost everything you can dream of – you can do it if you use vision. And here's the great thing: once you have set up the mental disharmony, you don't have to use your conscious mind to worry and plan how to get there; your subconscious will do it for you. You will still have to do the necessary work, but somehow you won't see it as onerous. Things will start to happen seemingly on their own, and you will be drawn into them with an energy you have not felt before.

The Dark Side of Vision

There is, however, a dark side to all of this, best summarized in this quote by Henry Ford: "Whether you think you can, or you think you can't, you're right." Remember, your subconscious mind believes everything is true. So if you say, "I just can't lose weight, I've tried everything," your subconscious is going to say, "Fine." If you make the same pronounce-ment about smoking, it's going to say, "OK, I'll make sure you don't quit smoking. I want to make the picture real."

I saw an example of this during a golf game. I was in a foursome approaching a 130-yard par-three hole, the first hundred yards of which was over water. I watched as my buddy teed up, stood over his ball, and surveyed the challenge. He looked ready to go, but just before hitting the ball, he changed his mind, replacing his ball with an old one he had found and kept in his bag, probably for just this purpose. If I had asked him, "What is the desired future state for your ball?" he probably would have said, "On the green." But the reality of his vision, shown in his hesitation, indecisiveness, and reliance on luck, was it was going to land in the water. Sure enough, it did just that.

I have read many articles about the PGA, often coming across the statement that most players at that level of the game can make a ball do just about anything. The difference between winning and losing for them is the mind and being able to control it.

The new science backs up these realities about vision. There are many phenomena of subatomic research scientists don't quite understand. One is that it is impossible to observe a subatomic particle in its natural state. Electrons are always moving, but we are unable to observe this completely. When scientists set up an experiment to discover the speed of an electron, that's what they find, but they won't be able to determine its location. If they set up an experiment to find the location, they will do so, but they won't be able to determine its speed. In other words, at the subatomic level, you get what you're looking for.

Look for What You Want

If this is true at the subatomic level, why couldn't it be true at our conscious level? I believe it is. I believe we can get what we're looking for in life by looking for it.

What is also critical to the science of attraction is that when you focus your mind on your vision, you automatically elevate your thinking to above the 200 level on the Hawkins scale. This gives you energy in your body and electrostatic field, and the positive energy entrains others around you. We will discuss this further in the third part of this book, where we look at vision and leadership.

To close this chapter, consider what several luminaries have said about vision:

Formulate and stamp indelibly on your mind a mental picture of yourself succeeding. Hold this picture tenaciously. Never permit it to fade. Your mind will seek to develop the picture.
— Norman Vincent Peale

If one advances confidently in the direction of his dream, and endeavors to live the life he has imagined, he will meet with success unexpected in common hours.
— Henry David Thoreau

The greatest revelation of our generation is the discovery that human beings, by changing the inner attitudes of their minds, can change the outer aspects of their lives.
— William James

If you can dream it, you can do it. Always remember that this whole thing was started with a dream and a mouse.
— Walt Disney

Anybody can do anything that they imagine.
— Henry Ford

CHAPTER 7

Live in the Moment

Once you have taken the steps of creating a vision and have begun to practice focusing on it, it is important to allow yourself the mental space for listening to the answers that will come. This can be very difficult if your mind is always occupied with "stuff."

So far we have been talking about our thoughts in terms of the levels of energy they produce. I would like to shift from that and talk about them in terms of the past, present, and future. In terms of time, where do most of our thoughts come from?

There was a popular beer commercial a few years ago suggesting that "life happens to us while we're too busy planning for it" (an obvious riff on John Lennon's observation that "life is what happens when you're making other plans"). In other words, we get so focused on what we want to have happen and worrying about what we don't want to happen that we don't relax and enjoy what is happening. (Of course, in the beer company's vision, you would be doing so with one of their beers clutched in your hand.)

How We Think About Time

When it comes to thinking about time, we all fall into one of five camps.

Those of us in the first camp focus on the good old days. The majority of our thinking time is spent on fond memories of how things used to be. Sometimes this is coupled with an energetic critique of the way the world is today.

Those of us in the second camp look back on the old days as not being so good. We make comments such as, "You people today have it easy. When I was your age ..." We go on to relate the great struggles of our lives, which usually justify how we turned out.

Those of us in camp three focus on the future in dark terms. The world hasn't been a kind place, and we see no reason why it won't continue that way.

Those of us in camp four think about the future, too, but in terms of positive dreams and hopes. We don't allow thoughts with negative outcomes to cross our minds.

And then there is the fifth camp. It is talked about a lot. Very few are able to stay in for any period of time. Those in this camp think about what is going on in their lives right now. People who practice this say they "live in the moment." They have learned to stop and smell the roses. They neither dwell on the past nor fret about things to come, and they seem to be much more at peace with what is happening in the now.

Imagine you are preparing for a dinner party. In the moment, you are cutting a lemon, but where are your thoughts? Probably taking you backward and forward in time:

*Did I remember to pick up the dill for the garnish? I hope
I bought enough salmon. Oh oh, the sauce on the stove is
starting to boil; I don't want to ruin it. I hope Bob and
Francine aren't late tonight; this dinner has to be timed
to perfection. Boy, I could use a glass of wine ... Honey
could you ...*

Before you know it, the lemon's sliced, but you haven't
really been there for it.

Some see this busyness of the mind as positive. After all,
our minds have a great capacity, and multitasking has
become a way of life in our fast-paced world.

But what if you're doing something more important than
cutting a lemon, such as spending an evening with your significant other? You would think you would want to be there
for that. If you look back, you'll probably have to admit that
for much of the time you weren't. These mental habits of
not being there when we're there are hard to break.

And when we are not there, we are not seeing the world as
it is.

Refocusing on the Now

In his best-selling book *The Power of Now*, Eckhart Tolle
suggests that allowing past and future thoughts to creep
into what we are doing in the present actually deadens our
five senses to the experience. If we are looking at a flower,
but our mind is having concerned thoughts about a meeting
tomorrow, we don't see the true beauty of the flower. Our
worry frames our experience.

Tolle suggests we can practice a process in which we recognize past and future thoughts, catch them, and refocus on
what we are doing in the now.

If you can do this for a few days (and I have), the world will begin to look very different to you.

In Tolle's book, a student says to a master:

> A moment ago when you talked about the eternal present and the unreality of past and future, I found myself looking at that tree outside the window. I had looked at it a few times before, but this time it was different. The external perception had not changed much, except that the colors seemed brighter and more vibrant. But there was now an added dimension to it.

My experience with Tolle's practice has had the same result. Recently I took a Sunday and made a concentrated effort to refocus on the now for the whole day. At first it was difficult, but by mid-afternoon I was getting the hang of it. By evening I was really into it and was beginning to notice more details in what I was doing and experiencing.

At around nine that evening, I walked past an open newspaper I had been reading earlier, glanced down ... and couldn't believe what I was seeing. The page was almost three-dimensional. It was not a page my eyes could glance over quickly. The words, the pictures, the ads took on a new perspective; in some ways they came alive and held my focus. I looked away and then back a few times but the page remained energized.

Tolle suggests that when we look at the present world through a veil of past and future thoughts, we are deadening our world and not seeing its true nature and beauty. He also suggests that with enough practice, we can see the world as it really is all the time.

Vision and the Now

Living in the moment is also very important in the context of vision. When we create a desired future state for something and say, "I don't know right now how this problem will be solved, but as with all the others I've experienced, I will get through it," we must clear our minds so the answers can come to us.

When do your creative thoughts, your answers, most often come to you? If you think back, it's probably not at times when your mind is occupied with other things. When I ask audiences this question, most agree it is often when they are falling asleep or waking up or in the shower.

How many times have you had an answer to a problem come to you in the middle of the night when you are drifting in and out of sleep? Usually it's an *aha* moment, and you want to wake your spouse and announce your brilliance. Instead, you say, "It's OK, that thought was so profound, I'll remember it in the morning." Of course it always slips away by then.

Why do answers come at these times? Because that's when our minds are the quietest, are most in the now. We are not complicating our listening time with other thoughts.

Professor Ap Dijksterhuis of the University of Amsterdam argues that our conscious mind has a very low capacity. Because we can hold only a few thoughts in it at any one time, it is only good for making relatively simple decisions. But the subconscious, in contrast, has a huge capacity, though we are unaware of it. If we let the subconscious do its work, it will handle the complex decision making for us. His lab experiments have so far proven this out.

Living in the moment not only will enhance your view of the world, giving you more moments in your life to thoroughly enjoy, but will also allow the silence necessary for receiving the answers you need for your vision to come true.

But how do you know when the right answers have come along? How do you separate them from all the other thoughts you're having? This is another time when the concept of higher-energy thoughts plays an important part.

Remember the quote from Oprah? "Think of the elation, the satisfaction, the joy!" she writes. What are these but the high-energy feeling we are supposed to attach to our visions so they will appeal to our subconscious?

That's how you will know the answer is correct. Your subconscious will attach the same feelings to the right answers that you attached to your vision. It will feed this attraction energy back to you, and you will know you are on the right track.

The Answers Will Come

"Patience is a virtue." How many times have you heard that phrase? Usually our thoughts when we do are, "Yeah, yeah, right ..."

Many times I have been impatient when answers to some of the steps in making my vision happen don't seem to be coming. I have had to remind myself to reframe the impatience to something like, "No, the universe is unfolding as it should – be patient."

Some answers to visions come quickly. I've found myself saying just the right thing at the right time to an audience whose positive responses were envisioned only the night before.

But sometimes the answers take awhile to manifest themselves. It took me 17 years from the time I walked into David Grey's classroom to become a good teacher myself. Hitting my ideal weight took time. Only after three months of visualizing myself at 200 pounds did I notice any difference in my eating habits.

So, be patient. Remember, the more often you spend time with your vision, the sooner the answers will come.

Envisioning the Future

When you do find yourself thinking thoughts about matters other than what is happening in the moment, at least make sure the thoughts are about a desired future state. By envisioning that future, and being in the now when you're not, you will find answers come to you from your subconscious mind without your having to worry about developing a plan.

There is an old saying: "Learn from the past, live in the present, imagine the future." It may not be easy at first. But just as in sports or any other physical endeavor you have ever taken up, or any habit you have tried to change, it will come if you practice, practice, practice. This one is well worth the effort.

CHAPTER 8

Look
Up

During the writing of this book, I was helping a group with strategic planning for a trade show. The issue was how to attract more people to the company's booth. In our discussion we were focusing on tactics: prizes for visitors, special show discounts, the usual details.

After listening for a while, one participant, known for his success in putting shows on, was asked what he thought.

"Well, all of this is well and good," he said, "but the secret is in the mindset – how you think about your success at these events. If you have the right mindset, the answers will come."

This reminded me of a one of the major *ahas* of my life. Again, it came from an unexpected source, in this case a helicopter pilot.

I had been with a group of consultants and bankers, working on the creation of a training event for tellers and customer service reps. The event was supposed to provide insights into and motivate better customer service practices.

After three days of research, deliberation, and creative thinking, we were stalled, with no brilliant theme or concept for the initiative.

At that point Phil Scott, president of the consulting firm we had hired to assist us with the process, reminded us of the concept of lateral thinking: the process of looking at your problem through a totally different mindset. He then excused himself, coming back a few minutes later to inform us we were going on a mystery trip.

The drive from West Vancouver to the destination took 40 minutes, amid many speculations about where we were going. Soon it was clear the International Airport had something to do with it, but not the main terminals most travelers are familiar with. Instead, we came to the peripheral airport buildings, those harboring related businesses, services, and rentals.

To our surprise, Phil dropped us off beside a sleek, state-of-the-art machine: a helicopter waiting to take flight. After we had strapped ourselves in and donned communications headsets, Phil told the pilot what we were trying to accomplish: to see the world from a different perspective. He told him to just fly and have fun.

In the first seconds of lift-off, I was preoccupied with fitting my headset. When I raised my eyes, I was shocked. A Boeing 747 poised to take off was directly in our line of sight. We were drifting directly across its runway. I finally got the words out and into the microphone.

"Can you do that?" I said.

"Do what?" the pilot responded.

"Fly directly across a runway with a jumbo jet ready to take off?"

"Absolutely. I've got clearance."

My next views were sideways, first from my right, then from my left, and then one that seemed close to being upside down. The pilot was flying us just off the famous seawall of Vancouver's Stanley Park, following its curvatures precisely, turning the helicopter sharply left then right, only a few hundred feet over the heads of the many joggers and cyclists on the popular ocean-side trail.

Then we flew over Lion's Gate Bridge into the inner harbor, stopping above the people on the deck of the Pan Pacific Hotel. As we hovered, I became engaged in conversation with the others, losing track of what the machine was doing, only to be brought back to reality by the pilot's question: "Does anyone get airsick?"

Suddenly we realized that while we were talking, the pilot had maintained his position above the Pan Pacific but had let the helicopter climb precipitously within its hover. We were now looking down at mere specks of people from a few thousand feet up.

Without waiting for our answer, the pilot turned the helicopter over sharply. The next thing I knew, we were diving straight down, the mere specks growing larger every second. My stomach was in my throat as the sea rushed up to meet us, then my throat was in my stomach as we pulled out only a few feet (it seemed) above the water and roared away like victorious fighter aces in a war movie.

"Can he do that?" I thought. "We just dive-bombed the Pan Pacific."

The next 20 minutes of our "brainstorming" were a joy as we flew over sights we had never seen from this heightened perspective. At one point we flew fairly slowly over a suburban setting, looking down into backyards previously considered private. We hovered for a few minutes over a particular house.

"That's my place," the pilot said with a twinkle in his eye. "I like to stop by every so often just to make sure there aren't any cars in the driveway that shouldn't be there."

As the hour drew to a close, we were in for one last thrill. We went out over North Vancouver and flew up one of the many river canyons in the area. Just like in the movies, we flew very quickly a few feet above the river, with the twisting, treed, rocky walls rushing past us.

At this point Phil said to the pilot, "So tell me, what is the single most important thing you have to do as a helicopter pilot?"

His answer was a bolt of lightning to us. But before I tell you his answer, you should know that as part of our research, we had spent a day "mystery shopping" in some of the bank's branches. We had gone through a wide range of experiences. One observation we had made was that while employees were serving us, they rarely looked us in the eyes. Their computer screens, their calculators, their paperwork, their co-workers – all of these seemed far more important to them.

"The most important thing?" the pilot said. "Looking up."

A helicopter's rotor is designed primarily for lift. That's what makes helicopters unique: their ability to go straight up. In order to move forward, the aircraft tilts slightly forward, nose down, providing some thrust to the rear. But this means the pilot and his gaze are also tilted forward and the natural line of sight is straight into the ground.

"In order to compensate for this," he said, "I have to always remind myself to raise my head, to look up. That's the only way you can fly one of these babies."

And looking up was the only way we would think from that point on about the program we were designing. Subsequently, 6,000 people went through the program and it was very successful, changing people's attitudes and creating a friendlier customer experience.

Looking up is necessary to ensure good vibes. As with flying a helicopter, life's circumstances often put us in situations where looking down seems natural. The security of our job is threatened, we lose a big sale, or we find that all the work we put into a project is for naught as the company shifts direction. All of these experiences, if we let them, can have an effect on our gaze. We have to keep reminding ourselves to look up.

Looking up is also the only way to ensure that the vibes we produce are of a positive energy. If you look up at the levels of consciousness above 200 on Hawkins's scale and project from there, your vibes will entrain others.

And remember, the levels above 200 are mostly about others, so you will be looking up at others more often. "You can never escape repayment in the service of mankind." I'm not sure who said that, but whether you are in sales or management, you know it's true.

There's another facet of looking up I want to share with you Through visions of a desired future state, we create our own reality. My reality of what a helicopter pilot was allowed to do with a machine was not his. He had created his years ago as a child, dreaming about flying them. He had gained the skills and learned the rules and the reality within them.

We can all create the reality we want for our jobs and our lives. There are many testimonials to this and quantum science supports it. The observer experiences what the observer expects. We get what we're looking for not only in subatomic research but in our own lives as well.

So, look up, and get your vibes up. That's the only way to fly whatever baby you're flying.

PART 3

Sales and Management Vibes

"No matter what a person's vocation or avocation may be, the nature of their progress through life is largely dependent on their ability to sell. And the most important things they have to sell are themselves and their good qualities."
— Frederick W. Nichol

CHAPTER 9

The Vibes of Companies

Later in this part of the book, I will apply what we've learned about vibes specifically to sales roles and to management roles. In this chapter, however, I will deal with both. That's because the two roles are usually played out within the context of a company, and companies can have a wide variety of vibes, some that will be congruent with yours and some that won't.

The Culture of a Company

The type of vibes a company has always comes down to its culture. If you think of the word "culture" from the perspective of social science, you can bring lots of images to mind. Some cultures are full of music, bright colors, and easygoing people. Others cultures specialize in stoic, purpose-driven, and serious people.

I once heard a cultural anthropologist introduce the topic to an audience by asking this famous culture question:

A farmer has two sons. To the first he says, "I want you to go and work in the field today." To which the son replies, "I will, Father." But then later he changes his mind and does not. He says the same thing to the second son, who replies, "I will not go, Father." Then later he changes his mind and does. Which son did what the father wanted?

The audience was a bit confused, but finally most agreed it was the second son, the one who said "no" but then changed his mind and went.

The anthropologist told the audience he had expected this answer because they were part of Western culture. "What gets done" is what is important in the West, he said. He said when he speaks to some Eastern cultures the answer usually is the first son, the one who said he would, but didn't. He said this is because in some of those cultures "harmony" is more important than what gets done. That his son was in harmony with him, in the moment, was more important to the father than what actually happened, or didn't happen later in the field.

And it's not just a question of East or West. Within one country there will be places where everything is easygoing and places where people are driven. Places where everyone knows everyone else and places where people haven't spoken to their neighbors in years. Some cultures are known for their art or their music, others for their science and industry. Some cultures are volatile, some placid.

Culture is formed when a group of people co-exist for a common purpose, creating norms, processes, and sets of feelings they all agree are important to live by.

One of the interesting things about culture is how people living in it aren't aware of the norms, processes, and feelings that constitute it.

Years ago I had the opportunity to work with Dr. Clotaire Rappaille, who has made a very successful career unraveling the secret archetypes of cultures for such companies as Chrysler, P&G, and Kraft. He says he knows he's on the right track when his clients say, "Wow! Oh ... I knew that."

He tells the story of a French cheese manufacturer attempting to broaden its market to America. France has some of the best cheeses in the world, but after two years of trying, they had gotten nowhere. They brought Rappaille in to see if he could unlock the mystery. He found that the North American cultural attitude toward cheese was exactly the opposite of the French attitude.

Children learn at a very early age about their cultures. French children learn about cheese at their mother's side when she is shopping. She goes to the cheese section where the cheeses are all laid out on tables in boxes. She selects one, smells it, and pokes it. "Hmmm, not that one." She prods and smells some others until eventually she says, "Ahhh ... this is the one" and puts it in her basket.

Without understanding it at the time, the child is learning that in France, cheese is a living entity. What the mother is doing is determining the age of a cheese. In France, you don't serve one that's too young or too old.

In North American culture, however, cheese is usually dead. In fact, in some states in the US, it has to be legally dead – pasteurized – before it may be sold. Once you know the archetype, it explains why we do the things we do with cheese. We wrap it in plastic like a dead body. Then we store it in a morgue – a cold place in the supermarket and our homes. It's dead and not going to change if we keep it refrigerated.

With this understanding, the French company developed a line of cheeses with French allure but that were dead and able to be marketed within the expectations of North American culture.

If you said, "Wow! ... Oh, I knew that" as you read the above, you understand the fact that we are not always conscious of our cultural norms.

Corporate Cultural Themes

Companies create cultures, too, and the energies of those cultures can differ greatly even when the companies are about the same size and are in the same industry. I had the opportunity to do culture work during the merger of two large financial institutions, TD Bank Financial Group and Canada Trust. It was fascinating to see that though both companies were successful, their cultures were very different.

One way to determine a company's culture is to ask employees to write stories about their experiences at work. I did this with people from both companies. They were asked to write about a day on the job in which they felt powerful emotion. The stories were very consistent but dealt with two very different themes.

In one organization, the primary theme was best characterized by this story:

> I had been promised a promotion but I did not get it. Rather than get angry, I decided to prove that they had made the wrong decision. For the next six months, I worked my butt off. On the day in question, the branch manager told me that he now realized that I should have been the one to get the promotion, and that unlike before, I would definitely get the next one. I felt *great!*

In the other organization, the stories were more along the lines of:

> One cold spring day an old man came into our branch shoeless and disheveled. We recognized him as a customer, but no one, including him, could remember his name. We made many phone calls, got other customers involved, and finally someone recognized him. We were able to take him home to his distraught family and they were very thankful. I felt we had really made a difference that day.

It was clear the vibes of energy in these successful companies came from different sources. Holding these two stories up against my earlier example, you could say one story focused on what got done and the other on harmony. Holding them up against the Hawkins scale, you could say one came from pride, level 175, and the other from a caring, people focus – one might argue from love, level 500.

The level of pride has enough energy to keep whole armies running, but which company do you think had a better reputation in the marketplace for customer service?

By the way, five years after the merger, the evolving culture has been able to retain the best qualities of both organizations. It combines a real customer focus with a get-it-done attitude, and customers, employees, and shareholders are very happy.

Understanding Your Company's Vibes

Whether you're in sales or management, it is very important to understand the vibes of your company's culture. If they are not in synch with yours and you are not able to adjust, it is not going to be very pleasant for you to work there.

From my experience, indicators of a company's vibes are revealed by asking the following questions. Hold them up against your company as you read them. Also be aware of your own vibes and compare them with the vibes in these examples.

What is the energy of your company's planning and forecasting cycle?

In some companies it is long and patient. For a fiscal year starting in November, planning begins in April. But I know of one very large company in which the first quarter has usually passed before plans for the year are finalized.

Ask yourself: What is my natural planning cycle? Am I a proactive planner, a measure-twice, cut-once person? Or am I more comfortable meeting the week's challenges as they come at me?

What is your company's energy cycle regarding its products?

In some companies, products have a long cycle. Payroll systems, operating software, passenger airline fleets, and large office buildings are purchased only after a lot of con- sideration. In other companies, these matters are dealt with on an "aim, fire, ready" rather than a "ready, aim, fire" basis.

If you are the type of salesperson who needs a daily hit of success and find yourself in the first company in this example, you're not going to be happy. If you are the type of manager who likes a slower, more thought-out approach to the job, you may not be happy in the second.

What is your company's capacity for having fun?

Some companies include "creating a fun place to work" in their official leadership requirements. Their conferences, celebrations, and daily work life have a lot of laughter in them. Other companies have a more serious, heads-down, and nose-to-the-grindstone feel to them. Again, do your energy needs fit the company and people you work for?

What happens to your company's energy level when the status quo is challenged and new ideas and approaches are suggested?

Do they go below the level 200, with pride in the old way of doing things preventing people from reaching levels of acceptance, willingness, and courage to try something different?

There are other indicators of a company's cultural energy: a focus on shareholders rather than customers, on product ingenuity or long-term viability, on long-term security or the ability to reap big profits quickly. All of these cultural norms will produce vibes in your company that you have to be aware of. If your vibes are not in synch and you feel you don't want to adapt to theirs, you will have a painful experience, probably spending most of your thinking time below level 200.

In fact, thinking in terms of entrainment can help you decide your career moves. If you are not in synch with your company, you may decide to stay and entrain others to your higher level of vibes. Or you may decide it's better for everyone, yourself included, for you to entrain, or be entrained to, vibes in a different culture.

CHAPTER 10

The Vibes
of Sales

It could be said that sales is the most vibes-intensive job of all. Energized salespeople and happy customers are a CEO's dream. But the reality is, a lot of salespeople have to drag themselves out of bed on a morning they have scheduled for cold calling, and a lot of customers will tell you they have been left with bad vibes after a deal was done.

Even those who thrive in the sales world think sales is one of the toughest jobs there is. Think about it. To be successful in sales you need to be a self-starter and a go-getter. You have to be positive and upbeat. All this when 80 percent of your time will be spent being beaten down. Salespeople on average hear 80 negative responses for every 20 positive ones. If you are not in sales, imagine spending 80 percent of your working day in negative territory. And don't forget, this is the average. For many products, it's even worse: 95 negatives to 5 positives.

I have spent many years teaching and observing salespeople and I firmly believe the ones who are successful have the innate ability to lift themselves up after 20 turndowns and go into the 21st call as if they had just made 20 sales.

I had a great deal of trouble with this when I was selling office equipment. Looking back, I realize why I, and many others, one some days just said "to heck with it" and spent the afternoon in a pool hall. The morning's turndowns had drained the energy from the afternoon's planned sales activities and we just needed to get away. This is common in the world of sales. We had to change pool halls whenever our supervisor located our current favorite. When I was made a sales manager at a new branch, the first thing I did was scout out the potential hiding places in my territory.

But now that we understand vibes thinking, a pool hall isn't necessary. We have talked about energized thinking and how to change our thought processes. Now let's look at making it happen in the sales world.

Create a Vision of Sales Success

When you get up every morning, do you think about how your day is going to contribute to your being in the President's Club? Do you create images of yourself winning sales campaigns and accepting the prizes? Do you picture yourself dancing with your adoring spouse as you sail the Pacific on the company Sales Success Cruise? If not, you should be.

We have seen that creating a vision is an important tool in creating life the way you want it, but in sales it is a crucial tool. If you don't think energizing thoughts, the 80 turndowns are likely to take hold and drain you. Every successful salesperson I have ever talked to has said a positive attitude is the cornerstone of their success, and the one sure source of this attitude is the vibes they get from thinking through a vision of their desired future state.

So when it comes to sales, create a long-term vision for yourself that has you getting lots of positive responses, winning, celebrating, accepting applause, spending, being promoted, whatever will give you the good vibes to sustain you through the down periods. Not only will it give you energy, but it will also lock in the cognitive dissonance that will get your subconscious working to make it happen.

Having a vision in sales is also critical for daily activities. I remember well my first attempt at cold calling. I was with the office equipment company, and it was a trial by fire. For one thing, I was still being considered for the job. For another, well, the first time out can be a nightmare for any fledgling salesperson.

As I said earlier, I had decided to go into sales to confront my stammer, but my sales manager had great doubts I would succeed. I was able to c-c-c-c-c-convince him t-t-t-t-to g-g-g-give me a t-t-t-try, however, and off we went. Cold calling.

I had a few lines to say: "My name is David Morrison, I'm with Olivetti, and we have a new calculator coming out next month. Could I bring one in to show you how it can add value to your accounting process?" I practiced it in my head as we drove.

He chose the office building and I chose the company. It was an engineering firm. When we walked in, the recep-tionist greeted us and I said, "C-C-C-Could I s-s-s-speak to the office m-m-manager?"

I'm over six feet tall, and the woman who came out was my equal. I can see her to this day with her stark gray hair pulled tightly back from a scowling face. Undaunted, I launched into my pitch.

As I have said, I didn't know any of this theory back then, but I do remember thinking I had to get this job because it was the key to my stammering journey. I also remember feeling and believing strongly that somehow I would.

"M-M-M-M-My n-n-n-name is D-D-D-D-D-D-D-D-D-D ..." (I had a lot of trouble with my first name and it's the one word I still stammer on today.) On and on I went and her eyes just kept opening wider and wider and wider.

When I got to the end and said, "S-S-S-S-So c-c-c-could I b-b-b-bring one in?" she said, "Uhhh, yes, sure, uh, sure, fine, yes, OK," as if she was in a trance. Later, on our way back to our office, my sales manager commented he wasn't sure what he had just witnessed, but he did give me the job.

Since I discovered the theories about vision, I have known that it and my subconscious mind's journey were to some degree responsible for my success back then. Today, I use vision for every sales call I make in my consulting practice. Before I go on a call, I picture a check coming in for the business I am pitching. I always arrive early and sit for 15 minutes, playing in my mind what I am going to say, and how the customer will respond, word for word. I picture the two of us coming to agreement as to next steps. I picture smiles, handshakes, and warm feelings all around at the end.

I have to say that, for the most part, the pictures come true, and they will for you, too. Try it.

Match, and Then Raise, Your Client's Energy

Now that you know what it looks and feels like to be thinking thoughts above the 200 level all the time, pay attention to where your client is. People usually find initial comfort when others match their level. People who are "up" like to be around other happy people. People who are down require a little commiseration before they are willing to move. As a salesperson, your job is to get them to, or keep them above, 200. That is where good business is done.

I've come across a number of techniques that work. Gary Fry (this book is dedicated to the memory of his son, John, who was living with me during the writing of *Vibes*, and was the perfect model of a good-vibes person) is very successful in sales because he consistently raises customer vibes with humor (appropriately of course) and by giving them something that's a little different, something they don't want to give back, as he puts it. A special pen, a little laser pointer, a yearly appointment book, and so on. "Nothing expensive, just unique, that they will remember me by with happy energy," he says.

Another salesperson uses the concept of dialogue in his sales interactions, the main idea of which is "asking questions to ensure understanding."

A consulting firm once videotaped boardroom meetings to determine whether dialogue or discussion was occurring during them. "Discussion" has the same Latin root as "concussion" and "percussion," both of which denote explosive negative energy. And that's what they found was happening most often. During hours of conversation, the number of questions asked was minimal compared with phrases like, "You don't understand – this is what our customers really want," and rebuttals like, "Well, according to my figures ..."

Discussion forces people into positionality. ("I'm right." "No, *I'm* right.") Positionality is present in all the levels below 200:

"I'm angry with you, because you ..."

"Can't you see that my way makes more sense than yours ..."

"You have embarrassed me and hurt my pride because ..."

None of this produces positive energy.

Never allow yourself to get into an argument or a debate with customers. Even if you feel you have won, in doing so you will have lowered their thought level to below 200 and left them with negative energy. There is, however, a strategy for ensuring that negative vibes will not drain the moment: approaching the customer from the perspective of dialogue, asking question after question to ensure understanding, and keeping the conversation up, at the levels of acceptance, willingness, reason, and courage.

Don't Take an "I Want Something" Approach

Salespeople and customers are always engaged in an age-old dance. Every salesperson knows the objective of any sales call is to make as profitable a sale as possible. Every customer knows this is true as well, and that the profit is coming from only one place, their pocket. They have also learned that salespeople, companies, and products don't always deliver on the promises they make.

In recent years, customers' fears have become heightened by the uncertainty of world and economic events:

- *"Will I make the wrong decision?"*

- *"Will a newer technology make what I am purchasing obsolete soon?"*

- *"Is this really the best deal, given all the many other choices?"*

- *"Should I be spending money at a time when the markets are down?"*

- *"Can I really trust this person?"*

A recent marketing survey reported that what customers want today is "trust and comfort in the familiar." The world is a violent and ever-changing place. Weary people want to find sanctuary in what they know and trust.

At the root of "trust and comfort in the familiar" is the word "familiar," which comes from the Latin "familia" or family. That makes perfect sense. Who are we more familiar with, or trust will be the same in the future, than our family? Even if there are things we don't like – such as when Uncle Henry gets loaded every Christmas, insists on carving the turkey, and then falls into it – we can at least trust it will happen – and become a family story that everyone will laugh at someday.

I read years ago of some research into a unique way of selling. The method was, in some ways, the opposite of what most of my sales courses taught, yet it worked. It won numerous awards, and ironically, it did not require cold calling.

As I was benchmarking this approach, I realized that the same elements making an impact in sales are present in a successful, happy family. The ones you read about under the 60th anniversary pictures in the paper.

Then, when I was doing best-sales-practice research for a major bank, looking at other industries, I heard of a woman, let's call her Linda, who had been extremely successful in selling a new technology, cellphones. It is ironic that today cellphones are practically given away. In the early 1990s, the first Star Trek flip-phone retailed at $2999.99, and even after you paid that much, the areas where it would work were very limited. It was not an easy sell for most, but it was for Linda. Let's look at the stages of a successful family and compare them to the approach she took to selling.

Stage One: Building the Relationship

The first thing that happens on a journey to a happy family, of course, is two people catching a twinkle in each other's eye. After that is the stage I call Building the Relationship. Lots of questions: "Where did you grow up, go to school, how many brothers and sisters, what do you like to read, eat, and relax at?" The more you find of interest, the more likely the relationship will continue.

And that's what Linda did in her sales efforts. She spent a lot of time early in the process asking questions and taking notes before talking about her product. She taught me that people are more than happy to talk about their lives if you just ask them in the right way.

Stage Two: Continuing the Relationship

The second stage of a happy family I call Continuing the Relationship. For a relationship to move on to marriage, the couple has to have aspirations, feelings, and desires in common. At this stage, people find out each other's preferences for how many children, city or country life, one or both parents working, religion, etc.

Linda did the same thing, except, of course, she focused on aspirations and desires for cellphone communication. "How often do you travel, how many calls a day to work, where do you travel, how critical is the phone to the way you do business?"

Apparently these first two stages took an average of 10 to 20 minutes each, and remember, she hadn't shown her product yet.

If you've ever taken a sales course, you'll know these approaches aren't unusual: get to know the customer and understand their needs. But the next two steps she took are the opposite of what many of us have learned.

Stage Three: Formalizing Expectations

The third stage of happy family I call Formalizing Expectations. That's what two people agree to when they get married. "I take this woman ..." "I take this man ..." Everything is positive, with relatives in attendance, music, good food, and that happily-ever-after glow.

What is not talked about, yet everyone at the wedding knows, is what happens when it isn't happily ever after, when the acrimony, the yelling and screaming, the crying, the lawyers, the divorce court, and the alimony kick in.

It's not talked about because it doesn't have to be. Everyone there knows what the downside to marriage can be – what can happen when you formalize expectations.

But does every customer know what the downside is to a product they are about to buy?

Heaven forbid, yet guess what Linda did? She brought the downsides right out into the open.

After finally showing her product and its features and benefits, and sometimes, just when the customer was ready to buy from her, she would say, things like: "Now you told me you travel the Toronto–Windsor corridor often. Well, unless you are right on the highway, you may not get a clear signal." Or, "You said you go to New York often – unfortunately, there have been some pirated chips so carriers are rejecting Canadian signals right now. I'm hoping it's temporary."

In other words, she made sure all expectations had been focused on – not just the positive ones, as most sales courses teach, but the negative ones, as well. In some cases, she talked herself out of a sale, but as you'll see, she was building customer loyalty and the future of her franchise. Just as the Bride and Groom do if they take their vows seriously.

I think part of Linda's appeal was that she stood out as a salesperson. To this day, I have never seen a sales course that teaches highlighting the negative, and I have never been involved as a customer in a sales dialogue that focused on the negative aspects of a product, unless I brought them up. But think about it, wouldn't you trust salespeople more if they did this? Wouldn't they stick in your memory?

Stage Four: Enhancing the Relationship

The fourth stage of a long-term marriage I call Enhancing the Relationship. It is about thinking of your partner first, putting their needs before yours. Looking for a way, every day, to add value to their life. Not taking for granted, once the vows are exchanged, that your work of strengthening the relationship is over. This is what takes a marriage to the 60-year mark, and this is the primary reason Linda never had to make cold calls.

Rather than doing so, she spent one-third of the time she was not with customers poring over the notes she had taken when she was in the initial stage of customer contact and finding out all she could about them. Another third went to reading business journals and magazines she thought would be of interest to her clientele. The final third was spent putting the two together along with a personal note.

"Hi, Jim. When we last spoke, you talked about a passion for fly fishing. I saw this article in *The Economist* about the growth of the private fly-fishing industry and thought you would be interested. By the way, if you're finding your initial phone bills to be a bit high, that's common at first. Give me a call and I'll help you with some ways to reduce your costs."

Linda spent her time giving to others altruistically, even when another sale to them in the near future was unlikely.

You can probably guess why she never had to make cold calls. It's the same reason another salesperson, in the home-entertainment business, never had to. I heard about him from a friend.

Mike was a stereo salesman and my friend was a high-end buyer. She had been saving for some time for her dream system and knew her stuff. When she went to the store, she was pleasantly surprised to find that Mike's technical knowledge was equal to hers. He answered all her questions and gave her what she felt was a fair price for the system. She found herself saying "Yes," a word any commissioned salesperson would love to hear on a sale of that many dollars.

To her surprise, however, he then said, "But just a minute, I want you to be sure. This company builds top-quality stuff, but they've been having a little trouble lately with tech support and warranty repairs. You said you need to have music in your life every day, and I would feel awful if system downtime caused problems. Usually they come through, though, and to be honest, their quality is so good that repairs are seldom required. Oh, and about compatibility with components of other brands, I don't know why you would want to interface, but some won't with this system."

She was dumbfounded. A minute ago she had been prepared to write a check for $20,000 and now ... After concluding that the concerns were within her comfort level, she signed the deal, but the experience left a good impression on her. It wasn't over yet, though.

The next thing that surprised her was his showing up on installation day, even though the company had sent a qualified crew. "His job was sales, and he wasn't getting any more from me," she told me. He stuck around and went over the instruction manual with her, then left once he knew everything was OK.

She said he called a couple of weeks later, but she saw that as a routine follow-up.

What made the biggest impression on her, however, was when he called four months later (she says at this point she thought he was looking for a date). This time he told her an obscure audio magazine had done a product review on her system. Had she seen it? He said he would be happy to drop it off the next week when he was going to be in her area.

Sure enough, he stopped in, even brought a little audiophile gift to thank her for the business four months previously, without even a hint that he wanted something more.

She finally "got it" when friends were over for a party, someone was admiring her system, and she found herself saying, "Well, if you're ever in the market, you just have to go and see Mike. You won't believe this guy."

Neither Mike nor Linda had an "I want something" approach to selling. I don't know if Mike was as successful as Linda was, but that's why she never had to make cold calls – she simply handled her referrals.

Just as in marriages and life, the highest vibes come from doing something for others. More importantly, those vibes attract others. Remember the people in the management groups creating models of doing something to eradicate hunger and poverty? Remember the vibes they felt?

States of consciousness below the 200 level are focused on self. States above 200 are focused on others. We are the happiest when we are thinking of and helping others. Put that energy, those vibes, into your sales calls, and you will create the success you envision.

CHAPTER 11

The Vibes of Management

I was working as a new sales manager in a large branch with 30 salespeople, divided into three teams, one of which was mine. Sales had been slow, and one of the other managers suggested we have a steak and beans contest. This meant nothing to me so I asked him to explain.

"It's simple," he said. "We'll challenge the other big branch across town to a three-month revenue contest. At the end we'll all have a big party at a steak house. The losers will buy steak for the winners, and the winners will buy beans for the losers."

At first this seemed silly to me. These are grown men, I thought, and he's asking them to act like adolescents. I sat back and observed others' reactions during the announcement meeting. I felt vindicated as 30 men groaned and snickered. I overheard some snide comments after the meeting was over.

And so we embarked on the journey. Not one of my choosing, but not one I could avoid, either.

At first things started slowly, with phone calls made to the other branch every four or five days, checking to see how things were stacking up.

A few weeks went by. Sales were slow and the branches were fairly even. Then the bombshell landed. The other branch received an unexpected order for a huge sale, almost an entire month's revenue in one hit. The news was devastating to my branch. Until then, the challenge had been a bit of a game. Now we were beginning to realize we might really have to eat those beans and take all the ribbing. That, plus the fact that the winners would be sure to choose the most expensive restaurant and order the biggest steaks and most expensive wines possible.

For four days, I observed the moping. "Management got us into this and management had better get us out" was the theme. But then something changed. People were huddling and their conversations were full of energy. I saw people helping others lift the heavy equipment into the trunks of their cars. (Believe it or not, some mechanical calculators with no more capability than one you could buy for $5.95 today weighed 30 pounds back then.) And I saw senior salespeople out on calls helping rookies in a way they had never done before.

The next eight weeks were nip and tuck, but gradually my branch began to pull even. At the end, however, with only a few days to go, sales fell flat. On the last day of the contest, we had a rally to pump everyone up and talk about pending sales that, with effort, might be brought in early.

It wasn't looking good. Then a man named Tenet Burnett spoke up and boasted that he would save the day. He had an order pending that would be enough and then some, he said. The problem was, Tenet often had big stuff going that didn't materialize, something the troops took into account as they pulled themselves up to face the day.

By 4:30 p.m., most of the reps were back. Close-off was at 5:00. Sales had been OK, but not enough to save the day. The men mingled nervously and I could tell they weren't looking forward to the call from the other branch. Then Tenet came in, walking three feet off the floor, arms outstretched, yelling, "I did it, I did it!" Skeptical, everyone gathered around, but sure enough, there on the bill of sale was a signature for one of the biggest orders in branch history.

The explosion of emotion was enormous. Men danced, cried, hugged, and yelled for five minutes. I'd never seen so much pure joy in accomplishment. Everyone had done his part, and Tenet had come through. The level of pride had been elevated to the level of joy, and that's a lot of positive energy.

Not only did it last through the next two weeks, until the Steak and Beans night, but it continued a good time to come. My branch set out to prove it was no fluke – that they could set records any time. A simple idea had leveraged the vibes of pride, with the vibes of the level of joy as the reward, and it energized people for months. It sure wasn't the steak, which turned out to be not that great.

Consistency and the Need for High Vibes

Looking back, I realize that this simple management intervention concerning a routine task had released vibes to these high levels. The energy we felt could have generated enough electricity to run the city of Las Vegas.

Getting people to the levels of pride and joy is the job of managers today. A lot of jobs now are repetitive and specialized. Workers doing these jobs can very easily become numb to the vibes of emotion. Sticking with sales, think about it: cold calling, generating interest, demonstrating capabilities, and asking for the order – these processes are repeated again and again, with 80 percent of the salesperson's time spent in negative territory.

This is the context in which management faces its biggest challenge: creating the vibes that will re-energize their people.

While a corporation that consistently delivers high-quality services and products is the dream of every CEO, it is managers who make it happen. Consistency in meeting customers' expectations keeps them coming back.

Future Imperfect?

The meaning of the word "consistency," however, has been evolving. It is important, if we are going to manage toward it, that we understand what it means today. To do this, we have to go back to 1987.

In Chapter 12 we will see that the world of change in business as we know it today began in the 1970s. Customers' expectations began to shift and corporations began to re-examine themselves. The primary driver of this change was new technology. Not just the technology that is electronic and mechanical, but also the technology of how things are done.

Most people associate technology with things, mostly electronic. But in the true meaning of the word, it is about how something is done. Prayer is a technology for getting closer to a God. Low-tech in this context is, "Now I lay me down to sleep." High-tech is becoming a monk or a nun.

In business, the technology changes of the 1970s and early 80s were certainly focused on computing, telecommunications, and robotization, but they also were concerned with continuous improvement (Kaizan), quality circles, problem brainstorming, and empowerment. All of these contributed to new ways of doing things and changed customer expectations.

In 1987, Stan Davis wrote a book called *Future Perfect*. In it was a prescription for business in the future. Davis said customer expectations were shifting. In the future, customers would increasingly demand things that were Anytime (whenever they wanted it), Anyplace (wherever they were), No Matter (the less physicality the better), and Mass Customized (customized for their individual needs).

To a large degree, it has come true.

With Anytime, bankers' hours, courtesy of technology, have evolved from 10–3 to 24/7. Pizza is delivered in 30 minutes or it's free, and we can produce our photos digitally within minutes (remember having to wait for days?). You can easily think of many more examples.

With Anyplace, we used to have to go to bank branches; now we click away from our den. What used to be department store shopping can now be done with a website and a courier service. And we can access almost all the information in the world from wherever we happen to be.

No Matter is a no-brainer. Just look at shrinking computers, cellphones, and cameras. The information stored in a hundred books can now be put on one CD, and even money is ceasing to exist, replaced by electronic payment technology.

Mass Customization is not quite as far along, but it will catch up. Dell Computers is a great example of this concept (and of Anytime and Anyplace, too). At Dell, your computer isn't built until you give the specs. I've read that shirt companies are experimenting with scanners that take in every detail of your body to ensure a perfect fit, and car companies are experimenting with on-line customer specs being fed straight into the assembly-line mainframe.

You really do have to know your customers' expectations, though. A bicycle manufacturer who had developed technology that would custom fit a rider to their high-quality frames, with finished bikes delivered to them within days, found they had to delay shipping to keep customers happy. Apparently, people who paid that much for a bicycle weren't comfortable when it showed up only a few short days later. They felt something so expensive should take a little longer to produce.

Many of these concepts have also become corporate and industrial expectations of workers. "Nine to five" doesn't exist any more. Today we think about our management jobs around the clock and many answer their emails at 10 p.m., from home (Anyplace). We are also expected to do more with less (No Matter). And the day when all managers had secretaries is long gone.

Wanted: Manager Vibes

For many employees, this major shift means that the same thing, at the same level of quality, is done repeatedly. Over and over again. This happens to the extreme in a manufacturing facility or a call center, but it is also true for a sales force, store clerks, accountants, and customer service reps. Consistency may be the key, but consistency, unfortunately, doesn't have many vibes in and of itself.

This is where management comes in. Managers have to find ways to attach high-vibe thoughts to the boring, recurring activities necessary to ensure customer expectations for consistency, because such thoughts don't come naturally.

It's called motivating. Every manager who has ever lived has struggled with it. No one has been able to quantify exactly what motivates everybody at once, because people are so different. But now we know it's the high-vibrational energy of thoughts above the 200 level that will do it.

As I've said, the job of selling is a repetitive one. Cold calling, generating interest, demonstrating capabilities, and asking for the order are repeated again and again, all within the 80–20 reality of the job. Management has to create the vibes that will re-energize things.

Shortly after I took a new job as a sales manager, I witnessed the effect of this kind of management intervention. The lesson was taught by another sales manager. He was newly assigned to my branch. I went into his office to welcome him as he was unpacking and setting up his desk. To my surprise, as we talked, he began to screw the mounting for a brass ship's bell on the wall outside his office door.

"What's this for?" I asked.

"Well," he said, "I'm going to expect my men to ring this when they come into the branch at night and have had a sale that day."

Again, in my naivety, I thought, "Right, like that's going to happen. These are grown men. I know these guys."

As in the case of the steak and beans scheme, I saw sideways glances as the team heard this idea during the manager's "Getting to Know You" address to his new team.

That night as I dealt with my own troops, I kept my senses tuned to what was going on with his. Silence. People coming in and filing reports as normal. Then the manager came out of his office and asked, "Didn't anyone sell today?"

Two of his men said, "Hey, I did."

"But I didn't hear the bell," he said.

Both salesmen stayed rooted to their desks, with sheepish looks on their faces.

"Come on," he said. He walked over to one, lifted him up by his shoulders, drunk-walked him to the bell and helped him ring it, and then said, "There, that wasn't so bad, was it?"

He only had to gesture to the second man before he got up and, on his own steam, reluctantly rang the bell.

During the next few days his people began to realize that if they didn't ring it, he would "help" them, so they gradually began to do it of their own accord.

Then one night the ring was different: not the light little ding of obligation, but booming, clanging sound of success. A hard-won, larger than usual sale had been made, and someone wanted the world to know. The noise attracted everyone, which increased the praise.

Within a few weeks, everyone wanted to ring the bell, my staff included. It got so that people who had two sales would delay their commission on one for a rainy day, just so they could ring the bell more often.

More than that, people began to develop their own distinctive ring and in it a clue about the size of their sale. It was as though the world of commerce had composed its own uplifting melodies.

And the effect didn't wear off; my reps were still ringing his bell a year later, when I left.

Something as simple as the ringing of a bell had unleashed the power of the vibes of pride and joy, a power that energized people for long after.

The vibes of sales and the vibes of some industries, such as car manufacturing, routine though they may be, provide for occasional excitement. It could be the closing of a big deal, or a gleaming new state-of-the-art production line that has just been installed. However, there are other places where the vibes of consistency can be onerous. They can be found in the back-shop administrative areas of companies, where invoices are paid, customer files are updated, information is keyed in, and paperwork is processed. These places require special attention from managers. They can be boring and depressing. In fact, I would go so far as to argue that the prevalence of these routine jobs today is what has led to the reality television phenomenon.

Who Wants to be a Millionaire?, *Fear Factor*, the American and Canadian (and the world) *Idol* shows – all of these are about real-life, real-time emotions, vibes. That's what is missing from high-tech jobs and that's what people need a shot of, every once in a while. People who spend all day looking at computer screens or processing information don't have an opportunity to be around much emotion. If they can't find it in their job, they'll look for it elsewhere, even on their television screens. Even others who are not in these types of jobs have had the emotion of human contact diminish courtesy of voice mail and email.

And don't forget, high-tech doesn't just refer to electronics. It can also refer to sophisticated ways of doing things physically. Outsourcing has become a growth industry as companies find state-of-the-art ways to get people to move information, then sell this back-shop expertise to others. Outsourced processing is very high-tech.

High-Tech, High-Touch

In 1984, John Naisbitt predicted this reality-show phenomenon, though not in so many words. His concept was called high-tech, high-touch. He said that technology takes away from human emotion (touch) and that the more high-tech the world became the more need would be felt for a high-touch balance.

The 1950s were a time when the technology of television began coming into homes. Prior to that, families spent more time together, talking and sharing the events of the day. Now, although a family might be in the same room, the medium of TV cut them off from each other.

This period of increasing lack of touch precipitated the hippy-led love-in, flower power, communal "give peace a chance" movement that followed a decade and a-half later.

In medical science, the ability to keep people alive longer with high-tech has led to the rise of the high-touch Dignity in Dying hospice movement.

Wherever high-tech rears its head without a high-touch counterbalance, people will try to create their own balance. The need for emotion, for vibes, is that great. Companies leveraging this concept move ahead of the competition. This is true even when it seems to happen by chance, as the following story highlights.

The Green Machine Man

Canada is a world leader in the adoption of high-tech electronic banking. One of the reasons is that the journey had a very high-touch start.

When the idea of automatic teller machines, ATMs, first appeared, all the research indicated that Canadians didn't see the potential. They couldn't envision the advantages of going to a machine instead of going to "Mary" – at the time the TV commercial persona of a bank teller at the largest bank in the country.

However, some of the banks decided to experiment with the machines. They saw the potential of fewer Mary's and reduced expenses, should customers ever change their minds.

As predicted, initial reaction to the machines was lukewarm – until a late player got into the game and changed the face of banking history.

The Toronto Dominion Bank was among the last to get involved because its leaders couldn't see a business case but decided to put a toe in the water just in case. Robin Korthals, president at the time, took a personal interest in the project. I asked him to tell me the story.

He said the competition's ATMs were not having an impact with customers. After thinking about it, his people at TD realized why. The other banks' machines were just that, machines, stuck in cold cement walls with nothing to add warmth or friendliness to the experience of using them.

The two people who were put in charge of marketing for the project – well let's just say they were "different" – challenged themselves to handle any task from an unexpected perspective. In this case 180 degrees different.

Intuitively, they went right to the problem: that people are emotional and that the new technology was emotionless. They decided to add some emotion.

The first thing they did was add emotion to the ATM's name. One of the early favorites was "TD Terminal 2000" (picking up on the popularity of the movie *2001: A Space*

Odyssey) and the ads would play up the electronic bells and whistles.

They said no to this and chose a more rhythmic, emotional name: The Green Machine (green being TD's corporate color). To compensate for Machine, which is high-tech, they created a Green Machine Man (think Michelin Man or Pillsbury Doughboy) with outstretched arms to hug the customer and a smiling face where the electronic keypad should be.

They created a Green Machine scarf promotion in which employees and customers got beautiful green scarves to remind them of the benefits of the new technology.

They also made a very funny series of TV ads featuring a troop of monkeys cavorting about while at the same time using the Green Machines effortlessly. The point being, "Well, if a monkey can do it ..."

The rest is history. They had added high-touch balance to the new high-tech world of banking and Canadians never looked back. Not only did TD customers flock to sign up for access cards, but those of other banks did as well. Before long, "Green Machine" became a generic term for all ATMs in Canada, much to the other banks' chagrin.

High Spirit

TD had added the high-touch vibes necessary to overcome the fear and lack of emotion that high-tech can bring with it.

In this example, high-tech and high-touch worked together to create an energy that couldn't be stopped. If you manage an area in which there is a lack of touch in most of the jobs in the area, you need to create touch if you want the same effect. One of the best ways to do this is to think of ways to inject "spirit" into things.

"That team has a lot of spirit" is a statement most sports fans immediately understand, but exactly what spirit is being talked about? The English language is one of the hardest to learn because of the fact that so many of its words have more than one meaning. We have buns made of bread, buns on women's heads, and sometimes we say people have nice ones.

Asked to define team spirit, sports fans will say:

- *They play well together*
- *They work hard*
- *They play hard*
- *They have fun out there*
- *They care about each other*
- *They celebrate their successes*
- *They don't dwell on blame*
- *They are continuously improving*

If you were asked what the energy level of a team displaying those characteristics would be, your answer obviously would be "high."

The English language has a lot of other meanings for the word "spirit." We spirit people away, we have spirit lamps and spirit of turpentine. The most common use of the word is seen in religious terminology such as seeking spiritual guidance and the Holy Spirit.

SPIRIT /spir'it/, n
A fundamental emotion and activating principle.
Animation in action and expression.
The vital principle or animating force within living things.
The state of a person's emotions.
(Hyperdictionary.com)

The connection between team spirit, department spirit, and religious spirit can be found in dictionary definitions such as the one above and in their direct correlation to the energy levels of thought on the Hawkins scale.

If we go back to the scale, we can easily see the states of emotion usually associated with spirituality – love, joy, peace, and enlightenment – are also the states producing the most energy in our thoughts and bodies, the highest vibes, the most spirit.

We don't refer to sports teams or departments as being loving, peaceful, and enlightened, but now we can see that the high level of energy in both department spirit and spirituality causes us to refer to both with the same word.

> *The general atmosphere of a place or situation and the effect that it has on people. Infused with spirit: "The company spirited him up."*
> *(Hyperdictionary.com)*

In order to create spirit in a department of high-tech workers, we can go back to some of the definitions of team spirit for the answers.

- "They have fun together." *How much laughter is there on a daily basis in your department? If there's not much, think of ways to make it happen. More importantly, get others involved. As we'll see in the chapter on leadership vibes, people usually know how to do what makes them feel best.*

- "They celebrate their success." *How often does your group celebrate? Usually there are lots of production targets for back-shop areas. Don't let the achievement of one slip by without marking it with an emotional event.*

Again, get your people involved; they'll know how they want to celebrate.

- "They don't dwell on blame." *If your people point fingers, stop them. It does no good and brings everyone's energy down below 200.*

- "Things are continuously improving." *Let that become a department mantra. People feel better when they're making things better. But one expression like, "That's not the way we do things around here" can shut it all down. Ban that language!*

- "They play hard." *Look for ways to have people play. Make sure, if you have conferences, that there's some playtime involved. Orchestrate some fun after-hour activities.*

- "They care about each other." *Create events that demonstrate this. Even a cake break on somebody's birthday goes a long way. For large departments, a cake a month to celebrate everyone's birthday for the month works fine.*

These might sound like extracurricular activities to some, something a manager shouldn't have to worry about, but in the world of high-tech consistency, they can be integral to your success.

CHAPTER 12

The Vibes of Leadership

During my career as VP of Learning and Development for a large organization, I was involved in many discussions about the difference between management and leadership in the corporate world. Some said there wasn't any, but I always argued that there was.

In this chapter we'll look at the rise of the need for leadership in business. This will help us understand the need for the vibes of leadership, the subject of the next chapter.

Leadership

With all the books on the shelves today addressing the issue of leadership in business, it is hard to believe that prior to 1980 there were very few. There was really no need for them.

After the Second World War, industry and commerce were taken off their war footing but took on a big dose of the military mind. Returning soldiers filled the corporate ranks with years of experience in the military way of doing things.

The ensuing militarization of the corporation was in many ways a continuation of the initial development of the modern corporation, which itself was based on military thinking after the First World War.

Determining rank in the forces is governed by span of control. A lieutenant has a platoon reporting to him and a general an army, with the levels between assigned to companies, divisions, squadrons, flotillas, etc. It became that way in business as well. Supervisors had 5 to 10 people reporting to them; managers, 10 to 40; assistant vice-presidents, 50 to 75; right on up through vice-presidents, senior vice-presidents, executive vice-presidents, senior executive vice-presidents, and vice-chairs, and all the way to the president and CEO.

The system is basically the same today, with one very large exception. Now everyone expects companies to be led by leaders, and expects everyone down the ranks to exhibit leadership, too. What caused this focus on leadership? The 1970s.

That Seventies Show

In war, battlefield conditions change quickly. Reacting to them requires that everyone understand the military rules of following orders. Usually there is no time to engage in discussion about what to do in a situation. The ranking officer is expected to make the call and followers are expected to execute the plan, no questions asked. The alternative is severe. There are many instances in which a wrong decision cost lives, but that was acceptable: it was war.

During the period between 1945 and the mid-1960s, not much changed in industry and commerce or the world. Any images I have of President Eisenhower during his eight years in office are of him bestriding the golf course. In the 1960s, companies did not factor interest-rate changes into their strategic planning. Rates were at 3 percent and had been since the end of the war.

Business processes had also remained constant. As a child, I had seen movies in which a manager was portrayed going about some of his duties. Arriving at 9 a.m., he would walk to his (always "his," then) glass-walled office, whence he could observe row upon row of people at their desks, heads down, working their in baskets and out baskets. His job was to understand and communicate "how things are done here," to monitor and correct exceptions, and to make sure new people coming into the department understood. Because things didn't change much, this meant a long (two martini) lunch and early departure for the golf club.

The military imperatives of following rules and observing spans of control lost their effectiveness, however, with dramatic changes in the business world of the 1970s. In that decade, all hell broke loose. Interest rates soared to 20 percent during the oil crisis, hippies started the demand for corporate conscience, and technology began its world-altering journey. That's when the world of change, in the modern context, began. The concept and practice of span of control began to crumble, and all the more painfully the larger the span.

The first problem was with changing customer expectations and the ability to act on them. By the time the front line understood them and the message went up through the various layers (each of which interpreted it to its own advantage), any decision that was actually made was redundant. The expectations had changed again and customers were going elsewhere.

This brought about the realization that decision making needed to be placed closer to the front line, to the people dealing with the customer.

The second problem was that change itself was not something employees take to easily. Just because they received a directive to do things differently didn't mean they would. Sometimes the new way threatened their abilities, sometimes their security and position, sometimes even their job. And remember, they couldn't be executed if they didn't comply.

This brought about the understanding that management in business was becoming more than monitoring the status quo. Now it was also concerned with helping employees deal with change. And that brought with it a need to understand the difference between management and leadership, because it is leadership that people seek when things in their world are changing, and it is leadership that can change the way businesses react to change.

When our world is quiet, when we have a secure job, when our family is happy and healthy, when crime and inflation are low, when the economy is booming and there are no potholes in the roads or our lives, we don't want "leaders" poking their noses in. "Just let me get on with my self-actualization," is the sentiment.

But when the opposite happens, when inflation is out of control, when the crime rate soars and our security is threatened on every level, that's when we turn to our leaders, whether corporate, community, religious, or political, and say, "Hey, what's going on? Why aren't you doing something about this?"

People only need leaders in times of change. When something happens to the group that it has never faced successfully before (if it had, there would be no problem, and managers could manage it), and everyone has a different opinion about what to do, someone has to take charge and deal with the situation. A leader.

Within a few years, the books on management and leadership began to flow and a whole new industry, that of the corporate guru, took shape. First Warren Bennis, then a flood of others, from Peter Drucker to Tom Peters to Henry Mintzberg. I was deeply involved in research into the topics at the time and I remember the new revelations well. One had a major impact on me, and I am going to use it to explain why I am making a distinction between management and leadership vibes.

Managers and Leaders

"Managers do things right, leaders do the right thing."

I'm not sure who first said it, but I'm sure many of you have heard it. I agree with the distinction. Managers make sure that things are done right, so employees and customers know what to expect in their daily interactions with the company and its products. Leaders do the right thing, in making people comfortable with the changes that need to come and the different way of doing things, and ensuring that they see their part in it.

Helping people see their part in coming changes is critical to helping them deal with them successfully. The popular book *Who Moved My Cheese? An A-mazing Way to Deal with Change in Your Work and Your Life* by Spencer Johnson makes this very clear. The book is a parable about little mice-like creatures who take on human characteristics. One day, their world changes drastically when the scientists move their cheese supply to another place in the maze. As they try to deal with the issue, their discussion takes on all the typical fears and emotions that change brings.

In the story, Johnson makes it clear that being able to imagine a desired future state is a key factor in change management. He shows how one of the little characters, Haw, gets past the usual reasons for not doing something new.

> [Haw] saw himself getting lost now and then in the maze, but felt confident he would eventually find New Cheese out there and all the good things that came with it. He gathered his courage.
>
> Then he used his imagination to paint the most believable picture he could – with the most realistic details – of him finding and enjoying the taste of New Cheese.

And of course he does.

Good leaders know what the issue is: that many people get stuck in their fearful thinking and need to be reminded and even helped to see how great the future can look, and how great they will feel when they are part of it.

Most of us need consistency in our lives. For example, we all have our morning routines. It would be very disconcerting for us, in getting dressed for the day, to open the closet door and find that our partner has "rearranged things, for the better" yet again. If you want to see temper tantrums and mood swings, just mess with people's patterns of having breakfast and getting out the door to work. If their paper isn't on the porch, and their favorite cereal box is empty, and their car doesn't start ...

Fear of Change

The consistencies in our lives ground us and give us structure. But most of us also need to experience the vibes that change produces. Very rare are the people who don't find it exciting to buy that new car they've been dreaming about, or take that exotic vacation they've been planning. They want to feel the energy from 200-plus levels.

Remember the old rule of 80–20? We wear 20 percent of our wardrobe 80 percent of the time, we make 80 percent of our profit from 20 percent of our customers ... For most of us, that's the ratio that applies when it comes to consistency and change. We want 80 percent of our lives to be consistent, and about 20 percent of it to be different and exciting. It's true some people want more change than that, but from my experience in the corporate world, I'd say they're definitely in the minority.

Another 80–20 rule for many today is that we spend 80 percent of our time, one way or the other, devoted to our jobs. While we may have achieved a comfortable 80–20 consistency/change ratio in our personal lives, in the business world we rarely have a choice. Company mergers, new operating systems, economic downturns, shareholder anger, all contribute to things being done differently at work, and we're expected to adapt. The ratio often hits something closer to 50–50. That's pretty dangerous for human beings. We have been programmed against this level of change.

To explore this with groups, I put them through a little exercise. Audiences have a great time with it. Try it with some friends.

I tell people to stand in pairs, facing each other a few feet apart. Then I instruct them to really get to know their partner, appearance wise. What is he wearing, how is he wearing it, what jewelry do they have on, what kind of glasses?

I then instruct them to turn their backs to their partners and change three things about their appearance. There is some hesitation, but then they get into it.

Having waited till most are done, I tell them to turn around, face their partner, and take turns determining what has changed. At this point there is usually a lot of energy in the room.

When the room has quieted down, I ask them how successful they were. How many spotted one change ... two ... how many got all three? As you can imagine, almost all get two and many get three.

After congratulating them, I tell them I want to find out how good they really are. I instruct them to turn away again and change an additional three things.

Most people are a little dumbstruck. They stand in silence, their backs to their partners, with pondering looks on their faces and slumped shoulders. They show very little energy. Some begin to make a move, but most remain bewildered. I ask them if they are having trouble with this part, and most say yes. I tell them they don't have to do it, and tell them to sit down.

When they return to their seats, I ask them three questions, the answers to which demonstrate how we have been programmed when it comes to change.

The first question is, "When I gave you the first set of instructions, to change three things about your appearance, how many of you began by taking something off – a watch, a name tag, glasses, etc.?" Always, 95 percent of the hands go up.

Usually a couple of people have moved their watches to their other wrist, or buttoned up a shirt or blouse, or moved their name tags to the other side. But most people start by taking something off, without even thinking about it.

In my experience, and according to the people who designed this exercise, this is the same initial mindset people have when they are faced with change in the workplace.

- *"What will I lose?"*

- *"What will I be forced to give up?"*

- *"How will this affect me negatively?"*

- *"I was an expert at the old system, people came to me. Why change something that worked so well?"*

All thoughts below level 200.

We are programmed this way because in primordial times a change in the environment could have dire consequences. It may have meant a saber-toothed tiger had just entered the scene. Humans learned to be cautious at first, to check things out before embracing change, and fear is a healthy way to ensure this. There may not be any saber-toothed tigers in the corporate world (although some would dispute this), but our instincts sure haven't changed.

The answer to the second question is even more profound, when it comes to understanding change in the workplace and the need for leadership. I ask, "When I gave you the second set of instructions, to change three additional things, and you found it difficult, how many of you turned to your new partner for help?"

At this point people look a little quizzical. Very few hands go up – usually none. They hadn't even realized they had a new partner. But I remind them that when they turned away from their original partners, most were then facing someone else's partner, just a few feet away. If they had solicited the help of their "new partner," solving the problem would have been simple. Body language and a few whispers would have communicated a strategy: "Here, you give me your watch and I'll give you mine, we'll trade name tags and glasses and ..."

In the corporate world we have been conditioned not to reach out to others in times of change.

- *"What if they reject my overture for help?"*

- *"Give you some of my staff's time? I don't think so."*

- *"I can solve this on my own. What if I'm seen as someone who can't cope with new circumstances, who can't figure things out?"*

I once witnessed a management type address a subordinate brusquely as he walked by: "Talking to Smith again are you, Sanderson? When are you going to learn to figure things out for yourself?"

Reaching out and getting involved with others at times of change can help greatly, and yet human nature prevents it from happening naturally. We get trapped in the vibes of lower-level thinking.

The third question I ask my audience is just as telling.

By now I have been sharing the insights for a few minutes with them, and I ask: "How many have already put the things you changed back the way they were?"

Practically everyone raises a hand sheepishly: wearing their watch on the other wrist just didn't feel right.

The Company Flavor of the Month

In an earlier chapter we discussed the discomfort people feel when changing their habitual way of clasping hands. Work habits are no different. When we are asked to change the way we do things, we feel the same discomfort, and the natural tendency is to work hard to get things back to normal.

Especially when 50 percent of corporate change is something most people have come to call "The Flavor of the Month."

The flavor of the month idea began in the ice-cream industry. Manufacturers and retailers figured out that a new flavor could capture customers' attention for 30 days. The term has become well known in business circles. It is applied to those corporate initiatives rolled out with great fanfare – a new way of selling, a new operating system, a different way of keeping track of customer contacts, a better plan for leveraging cross-business synergies – only to fall into the archives of company history as new efforts take their place.

I'm an ice-cream addict and have had my own experience with the Flavor of the Month concept.

In the early 1970s, Baskin Robbins introduced a new Flavor of the Month, Banana Bundt, and I loved it. It was a combination of banana ice cream, chocolate chips, and nuts – walnuts, I think. For four weeks, I stopped in every few days to reward myself when I had accomplished something. Then poof! Banana Bundt was gone. I asked if they might have some left in the back, but they told me I would have to wait – that with any luck it would come back again, which sometimes happened when a flavor proved to be very popular. If it continued to be popular, it might even make it into the hallowed 31 flavors. Jamoca Almond Fudge and Pralines 'n Cream had started this way.

Alas, Banana Bundt was never to be seen again. Not enough people bought into it.

The same is true in the corporate world. If not enough people get on board with a corporate initiative, it will fade, no matter how much corporate planning has gone into it. Meanwhile, the people who did embrace it will have spent a lot of energy trying to understand and adopt it into their work lives, all for naught.

As a footnote, although Banana Bundt never came back, years later Ben and Jerry's brought out a flavor that came to be known as Chunky Monkey. If you've tried it you'll know it is banana ice cream, chocolate chunks, and nuts. Close enough for me. Sometimes a new idea has to be given more than 30 days before it will take hold. And sometimes it will take hold somewhere else.

We need leaders because of the complexity of life today and because of the shifting sands of corporate styles and fortunes – all of which is driven by the shifting needs and values of customers. Leadership practices are essential to helping employees adapt to change in the work environment.

People don't naturally go to positive, high-vibe thoughts when they first hear about corporate change. They have to be reminded by a leader to keep an open mind. They don't naturally turn to one another for help in figuring things out; this has to be orchestrated by a leader.

They also have to be coached in the understanding that Flavor of the Month efforts are sometimes necessary as the company tries new things to meet the demand of changing customer expectations. The corporate flavors people buy into will remain until their usefulness subsides, but even when they do, those who have learned to be open to change will have developed abilities and skills to change-proof their careers.

The next chapter is about the leadership attitudes and practices necessary to raise peoples' thoughts above the 200 level and in doing so unleash the energy that will sustain them and have a positive effect on the changes required to meet the company's needs.

For some, my view of leadership will be a surprise. It does not fit the usual concept of who leaders are and what they do.

CHAPTER 13

Leadership Vibes and Vision

I do a lot of executive coaching, working one on one with senior people to enhance their personal and corporate development. I always begin each relationship by stating three leadership principles I want them to work toward. I have found that they catch most people by surprise. Now, however, with my understanding of vibes, I am even more convinced they are the right ones.

Follow Me?

When most people think of leadership, the phrase "follow me" comes to mind. They think of Churchill, Eisenhower, Trudeau, and Kennedy as examples of great leaders. "Follow me, men, we're gonna take the hill" or something like that is a line in almost every war movie ever made. A good friend of mine has learned another perspective on the phrase. He is a very good skier and ensured that his son grew up on skis. As often happens when student surpasses master, "Follow me, Dad" are now the three most dreaded words in his world.

The idea of following leaders is age-old. The irony is, with sustainable leadership, that's not what happens at all – in fact, the opposite is true.

Manager, VP, EVP, and CEO are all titles organizations can give out. The title of Leader, however, is one only followers can bestow.

I demonstrate this with audiences by asking them to count up all the people they have ever worked for, from their first supervisor at McDonald's to their boss today. For some it takes a little time, but the numbers usually range from three or four all the way to 20 or so. Then I ask them to separate those they simply saw as their boss from those they saw as a leader, and give me the ratio. I tell them to go by their own definition of leader.

The numbers that come back are typically 12 bosses to 2 leaders, 7 to 1, 15 to 4. This proves two points. The first is that being a manager does not automatically make you a leader. The second is that there aren't many of the latter around.

More importantly, the audiences, when asked for their definition of a leader, give remarkably similar answers:

- *"He helped me to understand I could do the job."*
- *"She took an interest in me and helped me learn."*
- *"He was always looking out for us."*
- *"She showed us a way that we could contribute our creativity to the cause."*
- *"I was a better person when I left his department."*
- *"He cared."*

Statements like these show why "follow me" is an illusion of leadership. In reality, people only bestow the mantle of leadership on those who take them where they already want to go.

That's what Churchill, Eisenhower, Trudeau, and Kennedy really did, and that's why they're remembered. In politics, voters elect people who will advance the voters' agendas, not the politicians'. If the voters find this isn't happening, the re-election of these politicians is unlikely.

This is why the three leadership principles I urge people to work toward are more sustainable. They are:

- *If you want to lead the people, you must learn to walk behind them.*

- *Leaders will know they have been successful when the group says, "We did it ourselves."*

- *You can accomplish anything in life, as long as you don't mind someone else getting the credit.*

These principles are far more in line with how long-term leadership really works. They allow followers to feel the good-vibes energy from thought levels above 200, the levels where human potential and growth and all the energy within them are unleashed. Did you feel a few positive vibes as you read them? Most people tell me they do. Remember, above the 200 level, the focus is on others.

Listening

How do you do it? The first step is to work toward being good at the most important leadership skill there is. I'm talking about listening.

Whenever I am working with executives going into a new role, I tell them that for the first couple of months I don't want them to do anything, I just want them to listen.

To listen to every employee, every customer, every peer, every boss, to everyone they can. Only by listening can leaders possibly take them all where they want to go in connection with the responsibility the leaders have taken on.

The second step is to take everything they heard and see if they can identify and crystallize everyone's desired-future-state comments. If you truly listen, I tell them, you will hear these comments clearly. Every employee has ideas for making things better, every customer would like to see improvement in something, and every peer and boss will have opinions on how your business could be run better. I tell these executives that as they sift through the ideas, they will see a common pattern. It never fails. The employees are all talking about the same desired state.

Seeing the End from the Beginning

In earlier chapters, we explored the concept of vision as a tool in personal development. For leaders it is absolutely critical. Once you have found out where everyone thinks they should be going, your job is to paint a picture of the common themes in a way that helps people "see" the end result.

I heard Tom Peters speak years ago about how a vision was put into practice at Federal Express. Fred Smith started the courier company because he listened to potential customers tell him that getting something across the country overnight was becoming important to their business. (Remember Stan Davis's Anytime, Anyplace premise?) He also listened to potential employees tell him it could be done. With that as the vision – "Anywhere in the continental United States, overnight" – he started the company.

A vision is a desired future state, not the reality of today, and sometimes it's easy to forget that fact as a company begins its journey or begins a new initiative. FedEx was no different. Sometimes it wasn't easy fulfilling the promise, but the employees never wavered in their belief that the company was serious in its vision commitment and that they could make it happen. The employees believed they could manifest the company's vision.

An incident from FedEx's early days demonstrates this power very well.

As Peters tells the story, it was late at night and a truck broke down, with one last parcel left to deliver. The young driver of the truck realized he wouldn't be able to fulfill the company's promise.

Most people in the same predicament would accept the reality of the situation and book off their shift. After all, on the journey toward a company vision, stuff happens.

As this young man was sitting and contemplating the situation, however, he realized he was beside a small airport. Some lights were still on, one of which blinked "Rentals." Over the fence he went. He rented a helicopter, got the parcel delivered, and fulfilled the FedEx vision. That takes a lot of courage from an employee at that level. Even if there had been guidelines for this sort of emergency, they probably wouldn't include helicopter rental.

Of course, when the invoice came in, Finance screamed, but when Fred heard about it he said, "No, the kid did the right thing. If we really believe that we are living our vision, and if there are no guidelines for a situation, he made the right decision. For next time we'll see if we can't figure out a less expensive way."

From that day forward, every FedEx employee believed the company was serious in its vision, and they made it happen.

Some business books are full of examples of the use of vision to create desired future states. A few years ago, Sears realized their current image was not working – they were losing the loyalty of women shoppers. As a result, Sears changed its vision and created the "Softer Side of Sears" promise for both customers and employees.

Harley-Davidson successfully changed its vision a number of years ago. As I heard the story, technically advanced foreign bikes were cutting into sales, so Harley changed its desired future state. They went away from selling motorcycles to selling the Harley-Davidson "Experience." A major part of this change was centered on the company image and all the products that went with it: the clothing, the customized parts, even the sound of a Harley. The company actually patented it. Anyone who wanted to use it had to get permission and then pay royalties.

Happier Happy Hours

I mentioned the merger of the Toronto Dominion Bank and Canada Trust in a previous chapter and the fact that five years later it was seen as having been very successful by employees, customers, and shareholders alike. One of the reasons for this was that Ed Clarke, the new president, created and communicated a very effective vision for employees and customers: "Building a Better Bank."

This may seem trite, but if you work for a bank, it might have a little more significance for you. Banking is a fascinating industry from one perspective: most customers love to complain about it. Exchanging money does something to a relationship. In Canada, in particular, there is a love-hate relationship that has gone on for years and is unlikely to change, unless someone can ever "build a better one," and that's where the emotion came from in his simple vision.

As I listened to this new leader speak, I realized that if this could be done, it would not only make the customers' world a lot better, it would also make mine a lot better. I thought about how people responded to me as a person working in banking. Meeting new people at a cocktail party was often not pleasurable for me. Eventually the conversation always got around to, "And what do you do?"

Any banker who has been asked this question knows the conversation has a better than 50/50 chance of going downhill. Sometimes it's a complaint about the way Aunt Agnes was handled. Other times it's a complaint about unfair credit practices or about bankers making too much money (the members of my Sunday golf foursome never let a week go by without making this comment). Although I was proud to be a banker, this was one aspect of the job I did not enjoy.

Listening to my new leader, I realized that the question we should be asking ourselves was, "What do we have to do to be able to say we were bankers, mention which bank, and then hear the response, 'Wow, what a great success story you are. You guys really did change the face of banking. People used to hate banks, but not yours, not now.'"

I held his vision of the desired future state as long as I worked there.

The other thing this leader did well, in terms of setting out the vision, was to provide some guiding principles along with it. Principles that gave broad boundaries to how the vision would unfold. Remember the delivery driver? He was empowered, but with no boundaries. It was a significant event in FedEx history, but a company with forty thousand people can't afford to have everyone renting helicopters every time things don't work smoothly.

Our leader was precise in his principles. Putting customer focus before shareholder focus was one, making every customer profitable was another. Simple ideas, but ones that guided us on our journey to the new merged organization.

Empowering the Vision

Guiding principles give each employee the freedom to make decisions in the moment that will further the vision. People who work at Disney know exactly what to do in the Magic Kingdom when a guest has a problem. They know the vision is "The Happiest Place on Earth" and, within their guidelines, they can act accordingly.

Giving employees guidelines and then empowering them to make the vision come true is what leadership is all about, not just at the corporate level, but for all the departments within. To a degree, every unit within a large organization should have its own desired future state vision, one in synch with the bigger picture.

It doesn't have to be a finely crafted, graphically enhanced message. A story is often told about Andrew Carnegie and the simplest vision possible.

Carnegie was visiting a steel plant in which a new blast furnace had just been installed. After inspecting the unit, he spent time with the men who were just finishing their shift.

One of the questions he asked was how many tons of steel they had poured during their eight hours. "Six" was the answer. He went on to ask other questions and said goodbye, but as he was walking away, he took a piece of chalk from his pocket and wrote a large number "6" on the floor in front of the furnace.

When the next shift reported, they asked what the significance of the "6" on the floor was.

"We're not sure," they were told. "The boss was down here looking at the furnace, asked how many tons we had poured, and wrote it on the floor. He didn't say why."

Without any fanfare, speech, or brochure, Carnegie had placed a very powerful vision in every mind on the new shift: the number "7." It was imagined but it was as real as if he had written the number. Of course the number of tons produced by subsequent shifts over the months went up well beyond six.

Remember from the last chapter that the natural reaction to a changing environment is fear of loss, loneliness, and discomfort with the new habits required. That's why leadership vibes are important. A leader who knows how to release the power and energy of good vibes in a company by dreaming about a better future and getting everyone else dreaming it, too, is one of the most important assets any organization can have. As the commercial says, "Don't leave home with out it." Carnegie didn't.

Conclusion

After all the years of trying to unlock the secrets of the energy of attraction, it is hard to believe how quickly the answers came to me, during the time it took to research and write this book. All the examples from my journey in sales, management, and leadership really happened, but like my initial journey with the power of vision, I didn't understand why they had the effect they did. Now I do. It is as if the secret to all the things I had been wondering about came together at once, in a blinding flash of the obvious.

There is a story told about Archimedes, the discoverer of the theory of Specific Gravity. (The theory explains why an ocean liner made of heavy steel doesn't sink.) He had been pondering the issue for quite a while but nothing was making sense. One day he found himself settling into a bathtub of water that was just a little too hot (we've all been there). As he eased himself down, he noticed that the water at the side of the tub rose proportionately. In that moment, all the theories he had been pondering and the examples he had wondered about made sense. As the story goes, he jumped out of the tub and went running through the streets yelling "Eureka," Greek for "I have found it."

Now that I have found it, I can't let it go. As I look back on all the sales and management people I stood in front of over the years, espousing "The Way Things Work" in these realms, I know I wasn't giving them the whole picture. Now I can.

Whether we're in sales or management or a leadership role, the positive impact we have on others stems mainly from the vibes of the thoughts we have with them.

Those who send out vibes of attraction, whether in the business world or personal life, will always attract people who want to be around them. We all know people like this. We can feel the energy they give off.

If everyone in sales and management gave off this energy, perhaps their roles would take on a new perspective, one contrary to the many cartoon strips making fun of people in those jobs (see Dilbert, Blondie, Cathy, and Filbert, to name a few). The new perspective I am picturing is one in which being in sales and management *is* one that young people aspire to. One that makes them feel good about the contribution they're making to the journey of humankind in the world of commerce.

So get out there and sell. Get out there and manage. Get out there and lead. By raising your vibes and the vibes of everyone around you!